Marino smiles during an exhibition against the Jaguars.

Avoiding a sack, Marino gets a pass off against the Jets.

The Miami Herald

Alberto Ibargüen, Publisher
Tom Fiedler, Executive Editor
Rick Hirsch, Director of Multimedia
Dave Wilson, Managing Editor/Sports
Jorge Rojas, Executive Sports Editor

Bill Van Smith, Deputy Sports Editor
Luis Rios, Director of Photography
David Walters, Deputy Director of Photography
Roman O. Garcia, Editorial Specialist

Content packaged by Mojo Media, Inc.
Editor: Joe Funk
Copy Editor: Greg Roensch
Creative Director: Jason Hinman

Printed in the United States of America

Front and back photo by David Bergman

Photo by DAVID BERGMAN

Marino waves to fans as he exits the field after a wild card playoff game against the Buffalo Bills.

Contents

The Marino Intensity:
Dropping back against the Colts.

Marino: What He Meant To Us

 By Edwin Pope

I still think – always will – Dan Marino would be wearing a Super Bowl victory ring if he had gotten a chance to play against the Dolphins' defense instead of the San Francisco 49ers' in that dreadful 38-16 hammering the Dolphins took on a foggy day in January 1985.

Thing is, it didn't take a ring to define Dan Marino. He was purely the greatest passer ever to play football. No ifs, ands or buts.

Others could handle the ball better. Others could step livelier, although Marino's tootsies were quicker than most people realized. But for plain passing, no frills, for the ability to clip either one of a grasshopper's wings – you name which one – with football laces from 20 yards, no one came close to Daniel Constantine Marino.

You really had to be on the other side to appreciate Marino's passing as much as it deserved. You had to be, say, Peyton Manning.

Manning is the man who eventually brought down Marino's one-season record of 48 touchdown passes in 1984. Manning's the one who once felt so terrorized by Marino's passes he wouldn't even take his head out of his hands. That was the day Indianapolis beat Miami, 37-34, in '99, Marino's traumatic last season. "Every time I peeked out," Manning said, "Marino was throwing the ball 15 yards on a rope."

Marino did that to just about everybody. He couldn't do it to the 49ers in that 19th Super Bowl because nobody in the whole league had a better defense than San Francisco, and just about everybody had one better than Miami.

But how often did you hear Marino complain about the failings of any other part of his teams?

He didn't beef when his defenses were about as tough as screen doors. He refused to belly-ache when the Dolphins running game was only a hope but never a fact. Once, after a late-'80s game in Tampa, I mentioned to Marino that they couldn't seem to get anything going on the ground, and he actually looked surprised, as though that was the first time he had thought about it.

His attitude was, if the job didn't get done, it was his own fault. It almost never was his fault, but that's how he looked at it.

That's what made him a mortal lock for the Pro Football Hall of Fame. That's why no other athlete has ever made a patch on Dan Marino in this part of the world.

Yes, it's a pity he didn't get that Super Bowl victory ring. But it takes nothing whatsoever from his greatness. When you're the best ever, which Marino was, it's yours forever.

And ours.

That's the debt we owe Marino, for giving us his greatness, for the mere sight of him flinging a football. ■

Thank you, Dan Marino.

Dan Marino

Road To Fame

 By Jason Cole

Published: Saturday, February 5, 2005
Dateline: PITTSBURGH

THIS ROAD TO IMMORTALITY IS QUITE SHORT.

About three blocks, in fact. That's the distance Parkview Avenue runs from where it intersects Boulevard of the Allies at one end to where it stops at what is now Dan Marino Field in the South Oakland section of Pittsburgh.

Along this street was everything Marino needed in a football journey that took him to the Pro Football Hall of Fame.

But before Marino, 43, became the awe-inspiring passer South Florida fell in love with 22 years ago on his way to 420 touchdown passes and a slew of other records, he developed his unworldly athletic gifts amid a series of small brick row houses in South Oakland, a working-class section of Pittsburgh.

Everything that made him great, from his stunningly quick and unique throwing motion to his nimble feet to his supreme confidence, can be traced to that short stretch of road. Or, as boyhood friend Larry Lamonde said: "He honed his skills on Parkview Avenue. Playing ball running in the snow, between the hedges and the cars. There was nothing else to do. No PlayStation and we only had three [television] channels.

"Sports was our lives. There was nothing else."

A CHANGING PLACE

South Oakland is changing these days. Students from the University of Pittsburgh and two other local colleges are encroaching, using the homes as rentals.

The old-timers are easy to figure out. They're the ones who still diligently shovel snow, cleaning their steps and the sidewalk shortly after it falls. Statues of the Madonna dot many of the front yards and porches. People in South Oakland may not have much, but what they have they treasure.

The field at the end of the street was renamed for Marino about 10 years ago. There's a sign on the next street over announcing, "Welcome to South Oakland, The Childhood Home of Dan Marino & Andy Warhol."

Bring up Marino's name and the faces light with joy.

"When Danny got married, we had his bachelor party over at one of the bars right around here," said Denny Schack, who lived next door to the Marino family.

"His dad came by and said, 'Hey, we're just going to get together with a few people over there, come by.' The next thing you know, the place is full. It seemed like hundreds, everybody laughing and having a good time. Everybody loves Danny."

To this day, in fact. The night before the Steelers hosted New England in the AFC Championship game, Marino made an appearance at Atria's restaurant in the city to help lead a toast to the team.

Among the other guests were a bunch of local politicians and even former Steelers linebacker Andy Russell, who was part of the four-time champion Steel Curtain defense in the 1970s. For all the Steelers cheers, the biggest commotion came when Marino was introduced.

Marino's father, known affectionately around the neighborhood as Big Dan, laid the foundation for his son's success. Be it taking his son down to the field to hit a hundred grounders or coaching him on how to throw a football, Big Dan was a constant.

In particular, there was the throwing motion.

Marino's motion defies conventional logic, but it makes sense. Most coaches teach kids to extend the arm. John Elway, Marino's classmate in the great quarterback draft of 1983, is the prototype, his long arm motion producing a breathtaking toss.

Marino is more like a piston, a minimal motion made

Marino celebrates as he passes for a touchdown against the Jets.

with astounding quickness. The ball would be gone before most defenders realized he was throwing. Even his receivers were sometimes caught off guard.

As for the feet, that's one of the most forgotten qualities about Marino. While knee injuries eventually ravaged Marino's one-time good speed, he still could move. Where guys like Elway ran into the open spots on the field, Marino could make a defender miss even if they were both in a phone booth.

Credit jumping rope on the garage roof.

Marino's home stands out from the rest for a couple of reasons. It's painted gray and is the only one with a garage in front. The roof of the garage is an extended porch. It was there that Marino developed the footwork. On many nights, he grabbed a jump rope and thwacked away for an hour.

"He was the only kid I ever noticed doing that," Schack said. "He just kept going at it for an hour straight. You could hear the rope in the dark."

THE PASSION

As many athletes have proved, skill is nothing without passion. You can't play football unless you love it. There is too much pain and sacrifice, like the night after a victory over Indianapolis in 1995 when Marino finished even though he had been battered.

His left hip was engorged with blood from a nasty bruise. He got up in the middle of the night to go to the bathroom, but passed out on the floor and had to be rushed to the hospital.

Marino never let on when he was in pain. At least not until 1999, when a neck, shoulder and back injury forced him to the sideline during a game at New England. That would end up being Marino's last season.

"I remember that to this day," former teammate Trace Armstrong said. "I saw him that morning and said, 'How you doin'?' He said, 'I'm hurtin'.' He never said that. I knew it was serious."

Where does that kind of love of the game come from? It's not just about competition, it's about something much deeper.

In Marino's case, football became the centerpiece of a glorious life. He started playing in grade school for St. Regis, the Catholic church directly across the street from his house and where he and wife Claire were married.

In college, the Marino house was where everyone would come Saturday after games. Mother Veronica would cook up a batch of spaghetti and meatballs and the players, including Pitt greats Jimbo Covert, Ricky Jackson and Hugh Green, would come by the dozens to the three-bedroom, three-story house.

To make room, the Marinos and Schacks would open the gate to their small patio backyards and share space.

On Parkview Avenue, everybody took care of everybody. If you had 10 friends in the neighborhood, you also had 10 more sets of parents. Marino's godmother still lives on the other side of St. Regis, less than a deep pass away from the old Marino place.

And when you are cared for like that, you grow up with confidence and the ability to love back.

Asked last week if he could always throw the ball so well, Marino was at first bashful. But then he smiled and said: "You know what? Yeah, I could flat-out throw it."

He then joked that he could have quarterbacked the semipro team his dad coached... when he was 10.

Said former Dolphins teammate Joe Rose, who caught Marino's first TD pass: "When I talk to my kid about confidence, I tell him about Dan. He's probably sick of hearing me talk about it."

But confidence is not to be confused with arrogance. In 1996, Buddy Morris needed a big favor.

Morris, now the strength and conditioning coach for the Cleveland Browns, went to Pitt with Marino and eventually was one of the team's trainers, helping Marino along the way.

Morris' daughter, Kara, now 18, will need a liver transplant some day. It has been nine years since the doctors told Morris that, but the initial shock was cause for frenzy.

Morris needed money for an emergency fund.

Morris called, hoping Marino might be able to help him with a fundraiser.

Said Marino: "When do you need me?"

Said Morris: "When do you have time?"

Said Marino: "Buddy, when do you need me?"

They set it up for Father's Day. Over the next two years, Marino emceed and other players paid their own way to Morris' small hometown of Sharon, Pa. The more than $100,000 raised still sits in a bank account waiting for Kara's surgery.

"Danny is the greatest, that's all I can tell you," Morris said, the words fighting through a lump in his throat. ■

Young Brett Berman clutches Marino rookie cards worth over $100 each in 1996.

Welcome to Miami, 1983

By Bob Rubin

Curiosity, a trace of apprehension, and a whole gang of happiness were the emotions that swirled through Dan Marino Thursday on Day 1 with the Dolphins.

"There's always apprehension with anything new you do, but I'm not nervous," said the No. 1 draft pick. "It's a good feeling. I'm elated over the opportunity to come to Miami and be part of a great city and a great team with a great tradition. It's an ideal situation. Now, I'm happy I waited around in the draft."

The only other time Marino was in Miami was the wet weekend in early January when the Dolphins beat the Jets in the AFC Championship game. He was the guest of former Dolphin star Nick Buoniconti, now a lawyer/agent, who made an unsuccessful bid to represent him. (Marino chose Marvin Demhoff, who also represents John Elway and Curt Warner.)

"I had a great time and was very impressed, but I was only here two days, so I didn't get to see the city," Marino said. "I'm really looking forward to meeting new people, finding out about the city and getting involved in the community. I'll be doing what I love to do in a great climate with great people and a great team. I couldn't be more fortunate."

All those "greats" might evoke a measure of cynicism – but not if you heard the boyish enthusiasm with which they were said. First impression of Dan Marino: A big, handsome, curly-haired kid; friendly, open and impossible not to like. He smiles a lot and laughs a lot, frequently at his own expense.

Marino wasn't yet through the runway leading off his plane from Pittsburgh when he found himself in the spotlight Thursday. He blinked at the bright lights of two television camera crews and grinned. As they lined up for interviews, one TV man said apologetically, "You have to run the gauntlet."

Other athletes might have winced at that prospect, but Marino grinned again. "I'm used to it," he said.

He grinned an hour later when someone yelled, "Go Marino. Go Super Bowl." out of a Biscayne College window. He grinned when someone else asked for his autograph.

In fact, the grin seldom left his face. He answered questions – some pointed – at the airport and later at Biscayne, where he met Coach Don Shula, his staff and the other draftees, settled into his dorm room and awaited today's physical before the start of a two-day, getting-to-know-you mini-camp.

In getting to know Dan Marino, you must know his roots. He was known as "Pittsburgh Dan" because he was born, raised and played ball his whole life in a blue-collar section of Pittsburgh called South Oakland, just five blocks from the Pitt campus. He chose sooty Pitt over the more scenic West (UCLA) and warmer South (Clemson) because he wanted to stay home.

Marino is a "Pittsburgh Guy." Pitt Coach Foge Fazio once gave the following definition: "A Pittsburgh Guy carries himself with an air that he knows what's going on. He smiles and has something nice to say about everybody. He can relax on either side of the tracks... but basically is a shot-and-beer guy."

Marino's dad works nights driving a newspaper delivery truck, and left notes of fatherly advice for Dan because their conflicting schedules left them little time together.

Sample: "The game of life is more important than any game."

Another sample: "Play relaxed and things will fall into place. On days when they don't, it's not the end of the world. You can't force success."

Which is exactly what people said Marino tried to do last year when he was intercepted 22 times and his touchdown passes dropped from 37 to 17. Though Pitt finished

Herald File

Dolphins owner Joe Robbie introduces the rookie quarterback in 1983.

9-3, he suddenly became submarino in the ratings of NFL scouts, though he had the same gifts that had made them drool just a year before.

BOMBS AWAY

One prominent rap was that he tried to force the ball deep too often – Mad Bomberism.

"That's fair to a certain extent," Marino said. "Early last season, our offense wasn't doing as well as it should have, and sometimes a quarterback tries to make things happen instead of being patient and taking what the defense gives you. But basically, my ratio of interceptions over four years (68 in 1,167 passes) is lower than most."

"If you're going to throw the football, you're going to throw interceptions. You can't worry about it because if you do, you're going to throw more. You have to forget about it and go on."

On balance, Marino thinks he had a good senior season. "At quarterback, people expect you to do well all the time," he said. "At times, I got down on myself, but I think I came back strong. In any case, I'm not dwelling on it. I'm looking at the future, and I'm very confident of my ability."

Indeed he is. Last September, Sports Illustrated quoted him as saying, "I throw better than anybody in college, and I can throw with anybody in the pros. There, that's what I think... Sounds awful, doesn't it?" Awfully brash, anyway.

"The quote was misleading," Marino said Thursday. "I said you have to feel that way. I felt that way, and I still do. I'm not ashamed of that statement at all, but some people take it the wrong way. It's just one aspect of the self-confidence I think you have to have."

Marino's self-confidence is never more evident than when he opens his mouth to sing. A Blues Brothers buff, he loves singing, but listeners say that singing doesn't love him. "He's so off-key and so loud, it's like someone screaming over 90,000 people," said a former Pitt teammate.

What about it, Dan? "I try," he said with a laugh. "At least I try."

BRADSHAW BOOSTER

Pittsburgh Dan's hero is another singer, Pittsburgh Terry Bradshaw.

"I've enjoyed watching him play, have had an opportunity to meet him a few times and really like him," Marino said. "I think he's a super player and a super person off the field, too, which is very important. He doesn't let things get to him. He's very relaxed. I'd like to think some of that rubbed off on me."

"But I wouldn't say I've patterned myself after him. I think everyone has his own style and personality."

Marino's individuality is manifest in his affection for jersey No. 13, which he has worn since he was a kid. "I thought it was unique and no one I knew ever wore it," he said.

He would like to become the first Dolphin No. 13 since Jake Scott, but isn't going to push it. "I'll wear whatever I have to wear."

On Day 1 with the Dolphins, Marino was just trying to fit in. He isn't looking to set the world on fire immediately as Miami Dan. He says he knows he has got a lot to learn, and hopes to learn it from David Woodley and Don Strock, whom he labeled "quality quarterbacks."

His immediate goals are just to "learn the offense, get the feel, get comfortable. I'm not going to put pressure on myself to play right away. That's not realistic. I'll just see what happens and hope to contribute somewhere down the road."

Asked if he had been disappointed over the diminished pre-draft ardor of the scouts, he said, "Not at all. I know what type of player I am. There are a lot of guys who were drafted in the 11th and 12th rounds and felt elated. I'm 21 years old and have an opportunity to play NFL football for a great team. How can I be disappointed?"

The Dolphins think they got a steal. Does Marino?

Grin No. 237. "If they say so. I'm sure they know what they're talking about." ∎

Photo by BRUCE GILBERT

The "Rookie" during his first day of practice.

The First Win

By Bob Rubin

Monday, October 17, 1983
NEW YORK

The Dolphins had two quarterbacks going for them Sunday at Shea Stadium – their own Dan Marino and Richard Todd of the Jets. Marino, a rookie, played like a veteran in his second start, continuing to make a mockery of all the conventional wisdom about the difficulty of excelling at his position without years of experience. Todd, a veteran, played like a rookie, which has become a habit when he faces the Dolphins. Something about facing the aqua and orange seems to rob him of confidence and composure, makes him uncertain, rattles him, produces mistakes that would get a high school kid's fanny chewed.

The numbers from Sunday's 32-14 Dolphin victory sing hosannas to Marino and dirges to Todd. Though he had no running game to ease the pressure (51 yards, 1.8 per carry), Marino riddled the Jets with 17 completions in 30 attempts for 225 yards, three touchdowns and no interceptions. Todd was a grotesque nine for 26 for 114 yards and five interceptions.

The Dolphins have intercepted 15 Todd passes in their last four games against him, all Miami victories. "It's not very good, is it?" said Todd in a Hall of Fame understatement. "I have no idea why. I'm not going to build them up and say they're supermen. It's just good play on their part and bad play on my part. I can't make any excuses."

The Dolphins pressured Todd Sunday, true, but he pressured himself more, and the crowd piled on. The Shea crowd, which has had a long-standing love/hate relationship with Todd, turned ugly early with deafening boos and pleas for his removal. They've waited years for Todd and this Jet team to live up to what has long been touted as Super Bowl potential, and with each failure the reaction is angrier and more vociferous.

Which, in turn, probably makes it even worse for Todd. He is very sensitive to criticism – he once shot a birdie at the home folk and sulked in isolation after his poor performance against the Dolphins in the AFC Championship game last year. The Dolphins are the team the Jets have to beat in the division, but Todd goes catatonic when he faces them. It adds up to your classic complex and raises the question of whether Richard Todd will ever lead the Jets to the promised land.

In vivid contrast, there is the seemingly limitless future of Marino, Kid Cool. It's not supposed to be this easy for a rookie quarterback – witness the troubles of all-universe John Elway with the Broncos. Marino says it isn't easy. He had been on the cocky side at Pitt until his disappointing senior season, and now you couldn't find a trace of braggadocio in him with an electron microscope. But with his poise and quiet confidence, the second-by-second improvement he has shown, the release that proves the hand can be quicker than the eye and the laserlike accuracy, Marino is looking more and more like a potential franchise. The 26 teams that drafted ahead of the Dolphins may be talking about the one that got away for the next 12-15 years.

Asked how he's doing what rookie quarterbacks aren't supposed to be able to do, Marino smiled and said, "That's not for me to say."

As a college junior, Marino told Sports Illustrated he thought he could throw with anybody, anybody in college or the NFL. Now he plays it humble, and wisely so. But if you could read his mind...

So let others say it for him.

Ed Newman and Bob Kuechenberg, the two graybeards of the Dolphins' offensive line, hardly go overboard about rookies after two starts. Newman tried

Herald File

Marino gets a congratulatory hug from back-up quarterback and mentor Don Strock.

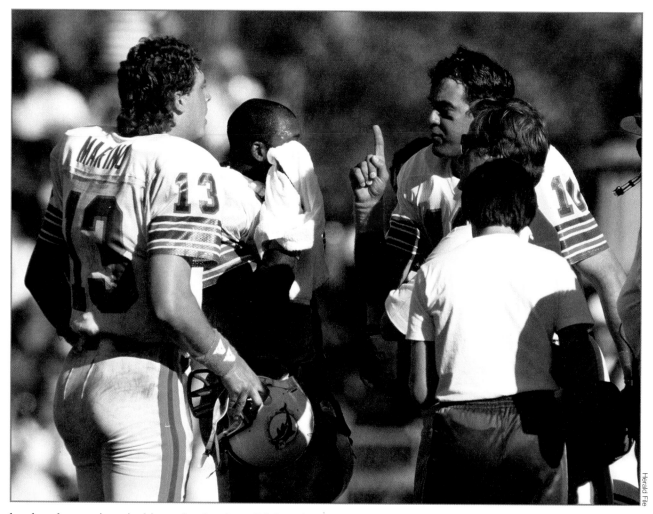

Herald File

A strategic consultation with coach Don Shula and Don Strock.

hard to be cautious in his evaluation but didn't quite succeed.

"He's got a long way to go," Newman said. "I don't want to canonize him yet. He screwed up a couple of calls from the bench and had to call a couple of unnecessary time-outs."

Then Newman grinned. "But whatever that magic quality of putting points on the board is, he's got it. He has no doubts about himself, never a trace of pessimism. It's certainly a pleasure playing when you don't go three-and-out. I'd say Dan Marino was a pretty good investment for the Dolphins and he's already paying dividends."

Kuechenberg was doubly impressed with Marino because he beat the Jets without the support of a running attack. "Thank God for that old whip back there," said Kooch. Old whip? An interesting slip, but under-

standable. It's Marino's head that's old, not his arm.

Kuechenberg was flat-out awed by Marino's 24-yard touchdown bullet to Joe Rose with 12 seconds to play in the first half, a score that gave the Dolphins a 20-7 lead and a fearsome head of steam going into the intermission.

"I don't think I've ever seen a pass like that," said Kooch, with the breathless hush of a fan. "Did you guys see it? One second he's standing back there and the next second, before you could say... um, Kuechenberg – the ball's in the end zone. I'm not used to seeing things like that on my side. It was all of a sudden – like whoosh." ∎

Photo by DAVID WALTERS

Marino acknowledges fan applause in a booming Orange Bowl near the end of his rookie year.

The Record 1984 Season

 By Greg Cote

On the radio, Prince was singing, Let's Go Crazy. Dan Marino was about to do just that. This was the beginning of Marino's second Dolphins season, and the beginning of the end for the NFL record book as we knew it.

For more than three decades the year already had been etched onto the national conscience as the title of George Orwell's famous novel about government oppression. Now, among South Florida sports fans, at least, the year would come to mean only one thing:

Marino.

Welcome to 1984.

In the book, Big Brother was watching you.

That football season, America was watching No. 13, the blue-eyed, 23-year-old prodigy quarterback for the Dolphins.

The curly-haired kid out of the University of Pittsburgh had had an outstanding rookie season the year before. He'd have 17 Dolphins seasons in all, in a historic career that put him in the Hall of Fame in Canton, Ohio.

It was that one 1984 season, though, that introduced Marino so spectacularly to the country and to the history books.

When it was over, Marino's NFL season records would include 48 touchdown passes and 5,084 passing yards. It was, and remains, the greatest individual season in NFL history. Marino's '84 would represent football alongside the best single years of Wayne Gretzky, Babe Ruth, Michael Jordan or anyone else.

Let's Go Crazy? Danny did, and right away, too.

The season went off like fireworks, with Marino's five-TD explosion against Washington in the opener. He completed 21 of 28 passes for 311 yards that day, with nary an interception.

"Everything happens like lightning," described coach Don Shula afterward, beaming and shaking his head.

Said a glum Redskins coach Joe Gibbs: "I thought we had a good secondary. But we hadn't faced Dan Marino."

It was only one game, but there was the immediate sense that something special, someone special, was happening.

"Everyone was talking about last year, that they didn't know if he could get any better," marveled receiver Mark Clayton. "He got better."

Said veteran guard Ed Newman: "I said last year, 'Let's wait and see about Danny.' Well, now we've waited and now we've seen."

The bombardment of touchdown passes and yards would continue unrelentingly, proving the opener to be not an aberration, but rather a harbinger.

Five times, Marino would throw for four scores, vs. the Patriots, Jets, Raiders, Colts and Cowboys. He would throw at least three TDs in 10 of 16 regular-season games. What Marino was doing made a mockery of that very phrase, "regular season."

Because this one was anything but.

That same '84 season, Walter Payton broke Jim Brown's all-time rushing record, Eric Dickerson broke O.J. Simpson's single-season mark and Charlie Joiner became the NFL's career leader in receptions. But all paled next to Marino's assault on the quarterback records.

This was the glamour position, and this was the new glamour player, electrifying America.

Marino's 429 yards in Game 5 five broke a single-game club record. By now, Shula's postgame summaries had become a march of adjectives in praise of the young phenom QB.

"What more can you say?" said Shula after that game. "It's tough to differentiate between sharp, sharper and sharpest..."

Barely past midyear, in Games 8 and 9, Marino surpassed Bob Griese's team records for TD passes and yards in a season.

Photo by JOE RIMKUS, JR.

Marino dodges the Raiders' Howie Long.

A four-touchdown Monday nighter against the Jets gave Marino 36 TDs and a share of the pro record George Blanda had set in 1961, and Y.A. Tittle had tied in '63.

"You've got to judge Dan by what he's doing now," noted Shula, "with the situation substitutions [on defense], with all these three-man lines and eight defending the pass..."

Marino would own the record all by himself one week later, though achieving it would be bittersweet, like much of his career.

The mark came in a loss to the Raiders, a loss despite four more TD passes that gave Marino 40. That same game, his 470 yards put him over the 4,000 plateau.

Some records are merely broken. When Marino took aim in 1984, records were smashed like clay pigeons struck by shotgun shells.

His 48 scoring passes were a full 33 percent more than the previous mark of 36.

By comparison, Mark McGwire's 70 home runs in 1998 beat Roger Maris' record of 61 by slightly less than 15 percent.

Marino's 5,084 yards passing surpassed the previous record of 4,802, set by Dan Fouts in 1981. Only five other men had ever surpassed 4,000 in a season when Marino set the new standard. He needed 256 yards in the season finale against Dallas at the Orange Bowl to reach 5,000. He got 340.

"Well, it's nice... real exciting for me to do something like that," said Marino in typical, understated fashion. "I never expected this kind of season. I just go with whatever happens..."

Since '84, the closest challenger to his yardage mark - besides Marino himself, with 4,746 in 1986 - has been Warren Moon with 4,690, nearly 400 yards shy.

Marino also set league marks that year for completions (362), 300-yard games (nine), 400-yard games (four), games with four-plus TD passes (six), and consecutive games with four-plus TDs (four).

So extraordinary were Marino's arm strength, accuracy and quick release, medical writers investigated to discern why.

Even before similar studies explored how Michael Jordan seemed able to hang in midair longer than a normal human, it was concluded Marino was blessed with more "fast-twitch fibers" than ordinary men. It was noted his right thumb was slightly broader and longer than normal.

Marino took the crazy adulation and the records in stride, always seeming to be mindful he was only 23, and crediting his teammates at every turn. Yet he exuded an unmistakable self-confidence, too, even a cockiness, that he didn't need words to express. He had this body language, an aura.

"He has this magneticism," said Newman. "This electricity in the huddle..."

Former Herald sports writer Larry Dorman, who covered the Dolphins that season, called Marino "the only man who can strut while he's standing still."

That inviting demeanor, his youth and good looks, the position he played and the records he shattered made an intoxicating cocktail. That Marino led Miami to a 14-2 record and into the Super Bowl didn't hurt. (Though the Dolphins lost, to San Francisco, Marino pitched eight more TD passes in three playoff games.)

Marino parlayed his 1984 into instant and huge stardom. He was the darling of the town and a budding national hero. He was a sex symbol as well, even though the news had leaked in November that Marino planned a postseason wedding with his college sweetheart, Claire Veazey.

Marino modeled fine suits in local ads. Pitched real-estate developments. Endorsed shoes, and gloves. Posed for a "Miamarino" poster that flew off store shelves.

"Dan Marino is easily the No. 1 football personality in the country," Marty Rosenfeld, a VP for MacGregor Sporting Goods, declared then.

A New York Times/CBS poll verified that, finding Marino to be the game's "most recognizable" active player. Second in that poll: Payton, who had just become the sport's all-time leading rusher.

So many other great Marino seasons would follow, enough to give him most every NFL career passing mark, too.

There was nothing else like 1984, though.

Not by anyone. Not before. And not since. ■

Very pleased with his young sensation, Don Shula offers some applause of his own.

Marino utilizes his trademark quick-release during the season-opener against the Chiefs.

Herald File

Super Disappointment

By Larry Dorman

Monday, January 21, 1985
STANFORD, Calif.

It had, of course, ended much earlier. It had ended in a barrage of San Francisco points that rolled across the floor of Stanford Stadium as inexorably as the fog that rolled in while Dan Marino was lying face down on the turf, recovering his own fumble when the clock ran out on Miami's season.

Face down. KO'd. That was, from Miami's viewpoint, the image to emerge from Super Bowl XIX. Dan Marino on the ground, the 49ers leaping and high-fiving around him.

San Francisco buried the Dolphins, 38-16, in front of 84,059 spectators and a national TV audience that undoubtedly had seen enough by the third quarter. On a Sunday that was anything but Super for Miami, the 49ers punished the Dolphins like no team has.

They sacked Marino four times for the first time in his pro career, held Miami to its lowest point output of the year and embarrassed the Dolphin defense.

Joe Montana, the Super Bowl MVP for the second time in his career, out-quarterbacked Marino almost as thoroughly as the 49ers out-played the Dolphins. Montana passed for a Super Bowl record 331 yards, he ran for 59 yards, more than any other Super Bowl quarterback ever has, and he threw three touchdown passes. He ran for a touchdown, too.

"He hurt us in every way possible," said Dolphin Coach Don Shula, pain evident in his face. "Every time it seemed we had some pressure, or every time it seemed we had coverage, he found a way to beat it. When you get beat the way we got beat, you take your hat off to the victor.

"I'd like to make all kinds of excuses, but I'm not going to do it."

It would have been difficult to find any that would wash, anyway, for there was no excuse for the way the Dolphins played. Marino was pressured all day, for the first time this season he threw more interceptions (two) than he did touchdown passes (one), and the San Francisco offense took the Miami defense apart piece by piece.

"Basically, we just went after them all day with everything we had," said Coach Bill Walsh, whose team's 537-yard output was the 49ers' highest total since 1961.

"I think we proved that a diversified offense that can move the ball on the ground and in the air might be more effective than an offense that leans heavily on the pass."

Certainly, that was true Sunday. The Miami ground "attack" produced 25 yards on nine carries. Marino's 50 passing attempts were the most in a Super Bowl since Ron Jaworski threw 38 times while his Philadelphia Eagles were losing to the Oakland Raiders in SB XV. Case closed. ∎

Photo by BILL FRAKES

A disappointed Marino sits in the locker room after Super Bowl XIX.

Watching the final seconds tick away.

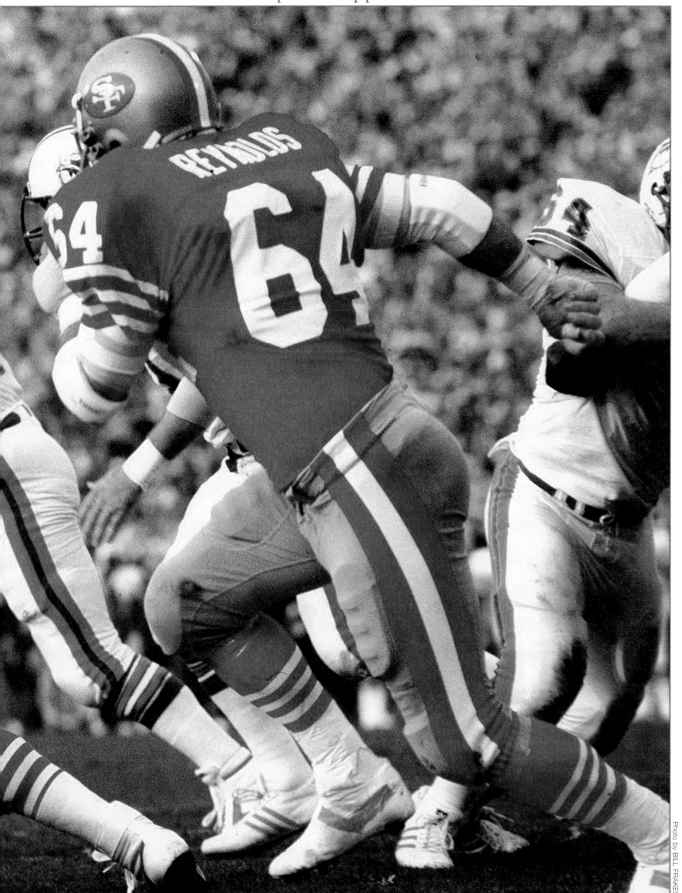

Scrambling against the 49er defense.

Marino – Elway I

 By Edwin Pope

Monday, September 30, 1985

DENVER

A man in a postman's uniform rushed up to John Elway in the bitter dusk of Mile High Stadium an hour after Danny Marino and the Miami Dolphins had shot down the Denver Broncos, 30-26.

"Take your picture with my little boy and girl, John?" the man pleaded.

Elway set down a small black duffle-bag in the bleak underhang of the South stands. He nodded wearily and posed with an arm around each child's shoulder. Elway even smiled, showing the teeth that a Denver newspaper cartoonist only Sunday morning had caricatured in a "comparison chart" of the celebrated Elway-Marino quarterbacking shootout – biggest teeth, ability to leap tall buildings in a single bound, and best-looking shoe being endorsed by the principals.

After all, posing for a picture beat running for his life from tons of white-clad Dolphin giants all the clattering afternoon.

And watching Marino pile up points.

Then Elway, the blond millionaire whose emotions at this point could have scraped a worm's underside, picked up his bag and started walking slowly away.

He stopped after two steps. He said one word, very softly.

"Marino."

Elway looked up at the dark sky. No one had to wonder whether he thought the word was a curse or a blessing.

"I'll tell you this," Elway said finally to one last visitor who wanted to shake his hand. "Marino is everything they said he was."

Bingo. Danny Ball is back.

The National Football League's season record-holding passer won the shootout hands down, 390 yards and three touchdowns to Elway's 250 yards and no TDs.

Strongest of all, Marino brought back Danny Ball with three of his best receivers out of action – already-injured Mark Duper and Tommy Vigorito and then Mark Clayton, sidelined just before halftime with a sprained ankle.

Most of Sunday, Marino was operating with wide receivers Nat Moore, who almost didn't come back this year; Duriel Harris, who came back only because the Dallas Cowboys didn't want him, and Vince Heflin, who was cut even by the Dolphins earlier this year.

"That's the thing about Marino," Moore said, inside the still-celebrating Dolphin locker room. "He gets the job done no matter how many people we lose. That's the mark of a true great."

Marino stood calmly in a towel wrapped around his middle and dismissed the Elway comparisons.

"John's a great QB," he said, "but this was the Dolphins playing the Broncos, not Marino playing Elway."

Yes, he said, he certainly did miss Duper and Clayton. "Believe me, I miss them. They can still get open even when they're double-covered. We threw over the middle a lot early when they were double-covering Clayton outside, and then when he got hurt, they started double-covering inside, too. But we've got so many guys who can catch, all I have to do is get it there."

That's nice, but not quite true. Dolphins dropped a half-dozen or so catchable balls Sunday, and Marino still rolled up his highest total since he struck the Pittsburgh Steelers for 421 yards in the AFC Championship last Jan. 6.

"Ron Davenport (rookie fullback) especially had a rough day holding onto the ball," said Coach Don Shula. "He dropped a pass and then he gave them that fumble before Denver's first touchdown.

"But, boy, Danny loves that challenge, doesn't he?"

On the practice field at St. Thomas University.

Meeting after a game for the last time in 1998.

Shula said. "I've never seen a guy enjoy competition as much as he does."

Elway relishes it, too. I think he is fractionally less accurate than Marino, but he's close enough to stand right on the golden edge of greatness, and he moves on ball-bearings, and he is going to be a great quarterback.

The Dolphin defense sacked Elway three times – Kim Bokamper, Doug Betters and Mack Moore.

Otherwise, they were chasing a ghost. But when a man scrambles as much as the Dolphin D forced Elway to, it has a tendency to disrupt the rhythm of his passing game. A lot of Dolphin secondarymen flying around helped as well.

I don't know if you could call this a game for the ages. But it was the most significantly positive thing that has happened to the Dolphins since they wiped out Pittsburgh for the questionable privilege of meeting San Francisco in the Super Bowl.

And Danny Ball did it.

It was a splendid football game for a lot of reasons.

It arrived as one crackling episode after another in the crisp weather that many non-Southerners feel belongs to football.

And the game absolutely rang with drama as the lead changed hands six times. The last change, Miami going ahead at 27-23 on Heflin's darting run with Marino's pass, won the game, but it did not end the drama.

Denver needed to go 97 yards in a minute and 39 seconds after Reggie Roby dropped a punt dead at the Bronco three.

The Broncs managed just 35 yards – 33 of them on three Elway passes – before Bud Brown swooped in and intercepted, and the lights went out for the Broncos.

Marino had faced a very similar situation just before half, and he handled it.

The Dolphins had third and seven at their 28 and a minute and 30 seconds to make 72 yards right then. And right then was when Marino ripped a ball nine yards to Joe Rose, found Clayton for the only time all day, and pumped a perfect 24-yard touchdown pass to Rose for a 20-14 lead.

Marino just whipped a stacked deck all the roaring afternoon.

This scrum was conducted on Elway's field and in his weather. That is, if 29 degrees and damp falling to 20 and damper is anybody's weather.

Elway had everything going for him – including a running game vastly superior to Miami's (169 yards to Miami's dinky 53) – and Marino and the Dolphins still handled him and them.

People tend to forget that the Super Bowling Dolphins actually won only one more game than the Broncos did in the last regular season. In Sunday's show, with all but the faintest touch of rust rubbed off Marino from his 37-day training-camp walkout, it was even easier to forget.

Especially for Elway, who ran and danced and ducked and dodged himself heroically into nothing more at the end than a bummer against unbeatable Danny Ball. ∎

Rivalry and friendship on the golf course after two Hall of Fame careers.

The Quarterback Class of '83: (from left) John Elway, Todd Blackledge, Tony Eason, Ken O'Brien and Dan Marino during the Marino farewell tribute. Jim Kelly, class of '82, sits between Blackledge and Eason.

Marino Preserves The Legend Of 1972

By Gary Shelton

It was there, in the hands of these Chicago Bears, like a golden treasure. And the Dolphins roughly, rudely and relentlessly snatched it away. Perfection. It is, after all, an adjective that belongs to the Miami Dolphins. And only the Miami Dolphins.

The Dolphins, resembling last year's AFC Champions more closely than at any other time this season, bashed the big bad Bears of Chicago, 38-14, in front of a frenzied Orange Bowl crowd of 75,594 Monday night in a game of playoff-level intensity.

Miami racked up 31 first-half points to bounce the Bears, including two touchdowns runs by Ron Davenport, two touchdown receptions by Nat Moore and one by Mark Clayton. Fuad Reveiz added a 47-yard field goal.

The Bears got a pair of one-yard touchdown runs by quarterback Steve Fuller and a 19-yard touchdown pass from Fuller to Ken Margerum.

They also got an NFL record for Walter Payton, who had his eighth straight 100-yard rushing game with 121 yards in 23 tries. Even that was cheapened, with the Bears trailing by 14 and rushing in the final minutes to allow Payton to get the record.

But they didn't get much else. For the Dolphins, it was an absolutely complete, absolutely perfect, domination.

There was no Fridge fun. William Perry lined up in the backfield twice, but the Bears ran quarterback sneaks each time.

There was no vaunted Bear defense. The Dolphins deep-sixed the 4-6. These guys could have been the Bills or the Falcons, the way the Dolphins went through them.

And, for the Bears, there is no more pursuit of history. The Dolphin ancestors of 1972 – many of whom watched the game on the sidelines – continue to stand alone as the only unbeaten, untied team through regular season and playoffs.

The crowd also deserves to divide a game ball. A dozen times, it forced Fuller to ask for silence. It was almost as rough on him as the Dolphin defense, which sacked him five times, intercepted him twice and forced him from the game with an ankle sprain early in the fourth quarter.

There was even more of a crowd than expected. A total of 75,594 tickets was sold, but with extra bleachers in the east end zone and fans in, as the Dolphins said, "bogusly," at least that many attended.

Previously, the Dolphin record for fewest no-shows was 284 last year against Pittsburgh. There were none Monday night.

The Dolphins entered the night in their healthiest condition of the season, and it showed. There was no intimidation by these meat-eaters from Chicago.

The offensive line more than held its own. And quarterback Dan Marino, with the time, was brilliant.

He hit 14 of 27 passes for 270 yards and three touchdowns.

The Dolphins showed early that no one, at least no one in South Florida, was afraid of the Big Bad Bears.

From the outset, it was obvious this wasn't going to be the slaughter many expected. The Dolphins treated the Bears more rudely than they had the Bills, the Colts or any other team in recent memory.

On the Bears' first three plays, they gained not an inch.

The Dolphins then took over at their own 44, and proceeded to dissect a defense that had dared to compare itself with the best the NFL has seen.

Remember, this was a Dolphin offense that hasn't been quite in tune all year. But the Dolphins scored 31 points in the first half, two more than the Bears had allowed total in

High-five from running back Najeh Davenport as Marino and the Dolphins preserve the unmatched 1972 "Perfect Season" record.

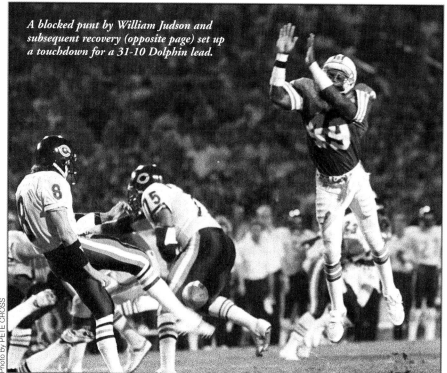

A blocked punt by William Judson and subsequent recovery (opposite page) set up a touchdown for a 31-10 Dolphin lead.

their past six games.

Miami did it despite putting itself in down-and-distance difficulty. On first down, guard Steve Clark was called for holding.

A minor inconvenience. On third-and-18, Marino rolled to his right and found wide receiver Mark Duper for 30 yards to the Chicago 34.

Two plays later, Marino sent Clayton deep down the left sideline, then found Moore circling underneath. He hit Moore at the 25, and Moore cut inside Leslie Frazier. Clayton gave him a block at the 15, and Moore went in for his fifth touchdown of the season.

It was almost possible to feel the Bears' shock. Linebacker Wilber Marshall pointed at Duper, as if to say he had been clipped.

In a way, the Bears' shock was understandable. They hadn't allowed a touchdown in the previous 13 periods or a point in the previous nine. In their previous seven games, they had given up only three touchdowns.

Chicago's offense acted as if it were going to make everything all right. On the Bears' first play from scrimmage, Fuller found Willie Gault streaking between the Dolphins' William Judson and Glenn Blackwood and hit him for a 69-yard gain.

Three plays later, Fuller went over from the one for the score.

Perry was in the game on the touchdown play, but it was soon obvious the same old Fridge fun and games weren't going to happen.

Lorenzo Hampton returned the Bears' kickoff from his end zone to the Dolphin 43, and Miami moved the ball to the Bear 30 before bogging down. Reveiz then drilled a 47-yard field goal, his longest as a pro and the team's longest since Dec. 16, 1983.

Four plays later, Fuller overthrew Payton on a screen pass and Dolphin linebacker Bob Brudzinski intercepted at the Bear 40. A personal foul against the Bears' Keith Van Horne moved the ball to the 25.

This time, it was Roy Foster called for holding. Another minor inconvenience.

On third-and-19, Moore made a twisting catch over Dave Duerson for a 22-yard gain to the 12. And after Marino was sacked for an eight-yard loss, he hit Duper for 17 to the one.

Three players later, Davenport knifed in from the one to give the Dolphins a 17-7 lead.

The Bears then rode Payton downfield on their next drive. Payton carried five times for 26 yards as the Bears moved from their 29 to a first-and-goal at the Dolphin nine.

But Fuller was caught in the grasp of Doug Betters for an eight-yard loss, and the Bears had to settle for a 30-yard field goal by Butler.

That cut the score to 17-10, but the Dolphins marched 79 yards for yet another touchdown.

This time, Clark was called for holding on the second play. Again, no problem. On third-and-13, Marino rolled out right and found Duper for 52 yards to the Bear 30.

All-Pro center Dwight Stephenson twice left the field with an ailing right shoulder, and twice returned. Without him, the Dolphins lined up with a patchwork line of Clark at center, Foster and Ronnie Lee at guards and Jon Giesler and Jeff Dellenbach at tackles.

That didn't hurt the Dolphins, however. And when Marino hit Clayton for 26 yards – 13 of them after the catch

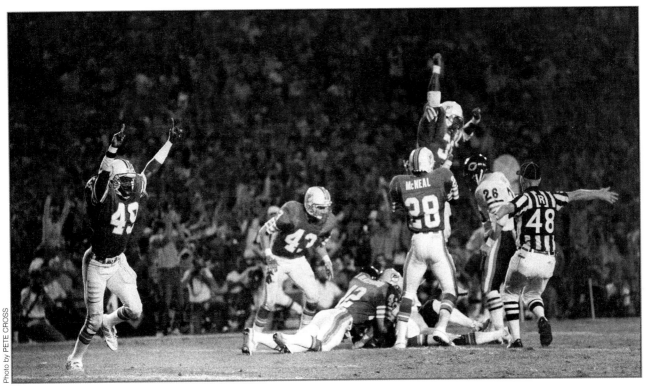

Photo by PETE CROSS

– to the Bear one, it was obvious these Bears didn't have their claws.

Two plays after Clayton's catch, Davenport went in for another one-yard touchdown, his 10th of the season.

By now, the Dolphins were cocky enough to call timeouts after Bear plays so they could get the ball back before half-time. And it worked.

As the Bears punted, Judson broke free up the middle past Jay Hilgenberg to block the punt and Robin Sendlein recovered at the six.

Two plays later, Marino hit Moore for Moore's second touchdown. Moore embarrassed Marshall on the play, and Reveiz made it 31-10 at the half.

The Dolphins gained 218 yards the first half, 194 of those on Marino passes.

The Dolphins finally had an unsuccessful possession as the third period began.

On the Dolphins' first play, Frazier picked off an under-thrown Marino pass to Duper, and the Bears set up shop on the Dolphin 43.

The Dolphin defense held, however, when Glenn Blackwood lept, intercepted a Fuller pass and barely got both feet inbounds at the Dolphin 10.

But the Dolphins turned the ball over again three plays later, when Marino found Clayton for 17 yards on third-and-10. Clayton caught the ball over the middle, but was stripped by Mike Richardson.

Richard Dent recovered for the Bears on the 27. A run of 12 yards by Payton and a pass of 13 from Fuller to Tim Wrightman set up Fuller's one-yard touchdown run.

The Bears attempted to follow with an onside kick, but Alex Moyer recovered and the Dolphins were in good field position at the 46.

Three plays later, the Bears returned to the 4-6 defense. And, on a freak play, the Dolphins returned to the end zone.

Nose tackle Dan Hampton deflected Marino's third-and-six pass, and it bounded high and long over the head of Richardson and into the waiting hands of Clayton, who turned and went in for a 42-yard touchdown. That made it 38-17 with 8:33 left in the third period. ■

Miami Dolphin Nat Moore catches a Dan Marino pass and runs for a touchdown Dec. 2, 1985 as the Dolphins met the Chicago Bears in the Orange Bowl, in Miami.

A Mentor's Respect

By Susan Miller Degnan

Tuesday, March 14, 2000

When Don Shula retired in January 1996, the quarterback he drafted and nurtured for 13 seasons was forced to ponder his own NFL mortality.

"I didn't think it was going to happen," Dan Marino said the day Shula retired. "You don't believe it at first and then to end it right now, I guess I was kind of in shock. The future will be decided later on, and right now everybody should appreciate what this man has done for all of us and for the players he has coached in the past and for this community."

The question surfaced immediately. How would Marino survive without Shula, the man who brought him to the doorstep of a Hall of Fame career?

Only four years later, as the 38-year-old Marino calls it a career himself, the answer is evident. Now it is Shula, 70, reflecting on his prize pupil, the piercing-blue-eyed man who blessed Shula and South Florida with a career that transcends even greatness.

"Dan Marino is the greatest quarterback of all time," Shula said. "I've always believed that in sports, people are judged by their accomplishments. Just look at those accomplishments. Look at those milestones. Look at those numbers. He has all the records."

"Some people say Dan isn't the greatest quarterback because he hasn't won a Super Bowl. But he has done everything else. One of the brightest parts of my coaching career was being Dan's coach for the 13 years it took for him to break all those records. It took Fran Tarkenton 18 years to set those records."

"Dan Marino is a guy who has so much pride and confidence in his abilities, a guy who thoroughly loved competing. Before every game I'd walk up to Dan while he was stretching on the field. 'How do you feel,' I'd ask him. No matter if it were snowing or raining, no matter what was going on in his life, he'd say, 'Great.'

Shula, who travels around the country overseeing the steak restaurants that bear his name, said he and Marino had a special player-coach relationship. Anything more would be unrealistic, he said.

"Dan and I had a great business relationship, because as a coach you don't really have a chance to be a player's friend in a buddy sort of way. Sure, we had our ups and downs, but anybody who has been in a relationship that long has had them. Dan has always been a guy you could depend on. Occasionally we talk; he called me to wish me a happy 70th birthday.

"The bottom line for Don Shula and Dan Marino: mutual respect."

Shula's most painful Dan Marino memory?

Photo by JOE RIMKUS, JR.

At a Dolphins practice at St. Thomas University

Photo by MICHAEL O' BRYON

On the sidelines against the Eagles in 1984

Both Retired: Marino gets a hug from Shula at Marino's farewell tribute at Pro Player Stadium.

"Not being able to get him back to the Super Bowl after he went to one in his second season."

Shula's best Dan Marino memory?

"All the great throws, all the great comebacks, combined. When he faked the clock play [against the Jets in 1994], his wonderful two-minute drives, Dan Marino being Dan Marino."

And Dan Marino being Dan Marino, Shula said, includes fathering three sons and a daughter and adopting a 2-year-old Chinese girl in December.

"He has matured so well. He's such a beautiful family man," Shula said. "He came in as a young bachelor and has grown into such a wonderful father. Dan talked about his family, but he never boasted. I'm very proud of how he has handled himself all these years."

Finally, Shula was asked if Marino could still play, or if he's too old to lead an NFL team.

"In all the years I coached him," Shula said, "he never had a sore arm. That pinched nerve [this past season] is the first [upper-body] injury I can remember Dan having. I saw him [this season] against the Jets and against the Colts twice. I saw him make some great throws, some great plays. Did people say he was too old after he drove against Seattle to win it in the fourth quarter?"

"The 13 years I coached Dan Marino," Shula said, "are 13 years I'll never forget." ■

Herald File

An injured Marino confers with his coach while recovering from surgery on his Achilles tendon.

Marino Shines Again – In A Record Loss

By Gary Shelton

Monday, September 22, 1986

NEW YORK

The Dolphins took one arm against a sea of troubles Sunday. That arm, the right one of quarterback Dan Marino, has never been better. But at the end of a wild Sunday at the Meadowlands, the arm was like that of a drowning man, protruding by itself above the surface as Dolphin fortunes sank.

The Dolphins lost in overtime to the New York Jets Sunday, 51-45, despite a career-high six touchdown passes by Marino, in front of a crowd of 71,025.

The Jets won when Wesley Walker caught his fourth touchdown pass of the game on the first series of overtime. He beat Don McNeal on a 43-yarder.

The Jets had tied the game as time expired in regulation on Walker's third TD reception, a 21-yarder.

The Dolphins had seemed in control when a three-yard touchdown pass from Marino to Mark Clayton gave Miami a 45-38 lead with 2:56 remaining in regulation. And the Dolphins had possession again with 1:57 remaining in regulation. But it wasn't enough.

The loss dropped the Dolphins to 1-2, with the San Francisco 49ers coming in next week to face a defense that has given up 101 points in its two defeats.

Dolphins' defensive coordinator Chuck Studley had no comment upon leaving the Meadowlands – or upon arrival in Miami. But Dolphin defensive back William Judson said that on the flight to Miami, Studley told the team, "A defensive player has to step forward and take charge on the field. We have to forget about it and come back strong next week."

But they will have to come back without outside linebacker Hugh Green. He will miss six to eight weeks – and possibly the entire season – with an injured right kneecap.

Yet some people still have to ask Coach Don Shula if he is concerned about his defense.

"Obviously," Shula said, rolling his eyes. "I already was, and now we've lost one of our best defensive players."

No wonder. If a quarterback can't win when he has the type of day Marino has, concern lives close by.

Marino became the NFL's all-time ratings leader at 97.152, passing the minimum of 1,500 career attempts to qualify.

He fired touchdown passes of six yards to James Pruitt, one yard to Dan Johnson, 13 and 46 yards to Mark Duper, one yard to Bruce Hardy and three yards to Clayton. Fuad Reveiz had a 45-yard field goal and seven extra points.

But New York quarterback Ken O'Brien also was superb. He hit Walker – who must have looked invisible to the Dolphin defenders – for touchdowns of 65, 50, 21 and 43 yards. Running back Johnny Hector, playing for injured Freeman McNeil, had touchdown runs of one and eight yards and Dennis Bligen had a seven-yarder. Pat Leahy had a 32-yard field goal and six extra points (the final extra point was not attempted).

In all, Marino and O'Brien set an NFL record by combining for 884 yards passing, breaking by one the previous high established by San Diego and Cincinnati in 1982.

"The offense did its job," said cornerback Don McNeal. "Dan Marino and the receivers did enough to win. We just have to start playing some defense. We have to stand up and be counted."

MARINO'S DAY ONE FOR THE BOOKS

Dan Marino's six-TD day is the NFL's first since Dan Fouts did it against the Raiders in 1981. Five QBs have thrown seven TD passes: Sid Luckman (1943 Bears), Adrian Burk (1954 Eagles), George Blanda (1961 Oilers), Y.A. Tittle (1962 Giants), Joe Kapp (1969 Vikings). ■

© Getty Images.

Marino displays brilliance but the Dolphins lose to the Jets 51-45

Earning Top Marks: Duper, Clayton

By Greg Cote

Monday, December 15, 2003

Smack in the middle of the Dolphins' December maelstrom tonight, smack in the middle of a game that could all but bury a season, there will be a few moments – just a few – to remember better days.

The present tense, the tension of Miami's desperate fight for any kind of place in the NFL playoffs, will lift and disappear for a while.

It will be 1983 again.

Mark Duper and Mark Clayton, forever The Marks Brothers, will be together on the football field once more. The man they will help deliver to the Hall of Fame, Dan Marino, will be out there with them.

There will be a highlight video, and it will be a time machine. It will show ghosts wearing jersey numbers 83 and 85 making magic, back in the day. And you could forgive a Dolfan, sitting in a stadium in late 2003, for wanting to close eyes tightly and somehow wish those two back

Marino with the "Marks Brothers" against the Chargers in 1988.

Photo by BILL FRAKES

into uniform tonight, as if they'd never left.

"I'm getting ready to suit up and go play against the Bills, like it's the 80s," Duper jokes.

Marino could make any receivers look good? OK. Sure. But it is every bit as right to say Duper and Clayton, together, took a gifted QB and helped dip him in gold.

"We are the two, right here, who put up a third of his numbers," Clayton notes, still with a cocky side at age 42 – but right on with the math.

Says Duper, now 44: "Clayton and I were very lucky to have Dan, and Dan was very lucky to have two receivers like us."

Deservedly, and at last, The Marks Brothers will be put up onto the Dolphin Honor Roll, the equivalent of the franchise's own hall of fame, in a halftime ceremony tonight. The club's record book has long known them as Marks of excellence. Tonight, they become permanent Marks.

"I felt pretty lucky to have two big–play guys, two guys as good as it gets in the league," Marino was saying the other day. "They felt like they could get open on anybody. I don't think we realized at the time the things we were doing, the numbers we were putting up."

Don Shula, professor emeritus in football history, calls Duper and Clayton, simply, "Better than anybody as a twosome," particularly mentioning the Steelers' Lynn Swann and John Stallworth, Hall of Famers both.

Can it really be two decades since Shula happened to draft a Northwest Louisiana track star named Duper in the second round in 1982, and then an overlooked Louisville wideout named Clayton in the eighth round a year later?

Was it luck? Serendipity? Shula magic?

Everybody said Duper was a "reach," drafted too high, a gamble. Heck, he didn't even know how to get into a proper stance at the line.

Photo by JOE RIMKUS JR.

For the Record: Marino gets a hug from former receiver Mark Clayton after breaking the record for most touchdown passes in 1995.

Right On Target: Mark Clayton pulls in a Marino touchdown strike against the Bills.

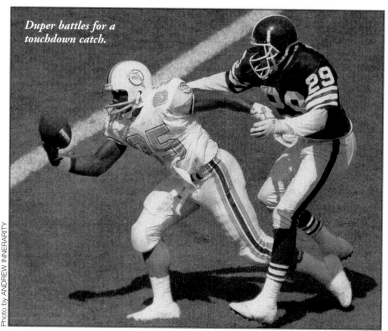

Duper battles for a touchdown catch.

Photo by ANDREW INNERARITY

eye – more lively to coach," Shula recalled. "Clayton was more apt to say something that might be annoying. But nothing that was disruptive. I can't remember much showboating."

Once, against the Bears in snowy Chicago, Clayton made a spectacular catch falling backward. The next day, in a team meeting, an unusually effusive Shula made a point of complimenting him on that play in front of the entire squad.

Clayton sort of sneered, and said, "Aw, it wasn't that great a catch."

Taken aback, then, Shula chuckles at the memory, now.

"He wouldn't even agree with me on that," said the coach.

The Marks Brothers retired in the early '90s as the two most prolific receivers in Dolphins history, a niche they maintain. Their career numbers measure favorably with many of the receivers in Canton, yet neither Duper nor Clayton has even made the Hall of Fame's final 15 in any year.

"But I'd seen him make catches in workouts that I'll never forget," Shula said. "The fear was he was a track guy trying to play football. But he was a football player with sprinter's speed. Short and stocky and powerful, with blazing speed."

Clayton was more wiry, not as fast, but with terrific, natural ability. A Dolphins legend is that Clayton could jump over a Volkswagen. Yet there had been 222 players drafted ahead of him when Shula chanced to spend a low pick on pure athleticism.

DISTINCT PERSONAS

Neither man was tall, but both seemed to find invisible steps when a pass was thrown high. They clicked with Marino right away. They grew up together. Their dazzle on a field matched their personalities off it.

They were not always the easiest guys to like. Or to coach.

Clayton was brash, a trash–talker, combative. He could strut while sleeping. Duper was quiet and could be moody. A reporter approaching either for an interview might find them welcoming and engaging, or not interested.

Their brilliance in games did not always translate to rapt attention in team meetings. Clayton, in particular, could get under Shula's skin.

"Duper was a wonderful guy, actually pretty quiet, where Clayton was more outgoing, with the twinkle in his

"The attitude, though seldom expressed, seems to be that it wasn't that hard to be that good a receiver when Marino was throwing to you," said The Herald's Edwin Pope, South Florida's representative among Hall voters. "I would hope either or both would be stronger candidates in the future."

Pope notes that players remain eligible for 25 years after they retire, so each has another 15 years or so of eligibility left.

A phenomenon of the process is that players who are not voted in right away, then seemingly forgotten, sometimes see their Hall chances age like fine wine. As an example, Dolphins guard Bob Kuechenberg did not make the final 15 until his 12th year of eligibility, then made the final six, and is today judged a strong candidate for induction when Class of 2004 results are announced during Super Bowl Week.

So Duper and Clayton still have a fighting chance for Canton, if not a great one. Making the equivalent of their own franchise's hall of fame, tonight, can't hurt.

"If they measure up, they should be in there," says the bottom–line Shula. "Look at it objectively." ■

Photo by JOE RIMKUS JR.

Clayton gives a Patriot defender the brush-off

THE
MUSICIANS
OF THE
PHILHARMONIC
PHILHARMONIC
MUSICIANS,
MEMBERS OF
LOCAL 655 A.F. of M.
SUPPORT
MIAMI DOLPHINS
AND THE NFLPA
HARMONIC
USICIANS
PPORT THE
LPHINS
AYERS

Dan walks the line. Marino, a member of the NFL Player's Association, picketed replacement players during the 1987 strike.

NATIONAL FOOTBALL LEAGUE
PLAYERS

ON STRIKE
or Fair
layer Contracts

For Better Pension
For All Players,
1920 Through 1990

NATIONAL FOOTBALL LEAGUE
PLAYERS

On Strike
To Honor

A Commitment
To NFL Players
Past, Present,
Future

Marino leads a meeting with locked-out Dolphin players.

A Big Playoff Win

 By Greg Cote

Monday, January 11, 1993

This game began like so many others this season for Dan Marino, only wetter. Nothing was working for the quarterback and his Dolphin offense through the first quarter. Punt, punt, punt, punt. Rain, rain, rain, rain.

You got the feeling this would not abate – this rain, this offensive drought – and that Marino would be asked to pull one more miraculous late rally from thin air, through raindrops this time.

On the sideline, when the Chargers had possession, Marino kept throwing practice balls, trying to get the feel, trying to coax a decent spiral from a stubborn, soggy ball. For him this is unusual. Was the ball slippery, Dan?

"I would imagine," came his postgame answer to such an obvious question.

But something magical happened as the second quarter began. Something very different for this Miami offense.

"Touchdowns," Marino said. "That was the difference. Just touchdowns. We scored touchdowns."

Water for the thirsty.

Marino and Miami had produced only six offensive TDs in 6 3/4 games before bunching three in the second quarter of Sunday's 31–0 playoff rout of San Diego at Joe Robbie Stadium. No Dolphins team had scored that many points in one playoff quarter, or fashioned so great a winning margin in a postseason game.

The offense, like the weather, came in a torrent. The defense played like a dam. The combination puts Miami in this Sunday's AFC Championship game against (who else?) Buffalo at JRS.

No matter that turnovers helped set up most of Miami's points. Marino had to finish the job; finishing has been tough this season. Not since Oct. 18 had Marino made a scoreboard light up like this. Not since then had he spun three TD passes in one game.

His statistics were otherwise not extraordinary: 17 of 29, 167 yards. But his performance in this weather was. His team's performance was.

"It's kind of nice to know we can win by 31, not just the close ones," Marino said, smiling. "That's satisfying a little bit."

Now, one more victory and there will be a game to play in Pasadena, Calif. A Super Bowl. Marino hasn't been in one of those since 1985, a million years ago.

Marino doesn't especially like to talk about how close it is now, and what that feels like to a man who has been waiting so long. Say the secret words – Super Bowl – and Marino answers politely and moves as quickly from the subject as he does from a defender bent on a sack.

"Two more wins and we win it all," he said Sunday, almost hesitantly. Then, like a superstitious pitcher being asked about a no–hitter in the seventh inning, Marino hastened to add: "We're not there yet."

Marino got poked in the left eye in the second quarter, but that was OK, because the points had begun by then.

"No problem. I think I just got some dirt in it," Marino said. ■

Marino fires from the pocket against the Chargers.

Marino Injured

 By Greg Cote

Tuesday, Oct. 12, 1993

We have not seen the last of Dan Marino. He will be back next season and he will be as good as ever. It is what the doctors are saying, and it is what Coach Don Shula is saying he believes, and it is what Dolfans everywhere are trying to believe.

But will he? Will he really?

Monday's news was as bad as feared. Marino suffered a "complete rupture" of his right Achilles' tendon during Sunday's victory at Cleveland. Surgery went well; still, rehabilitation is estimated at four to six months.

"Doctors felt good about the repair," Shula said. "They say the prognosis is good for a complete recovery."

I hope it is true, and any football fan anywhere should, too. Center Jeff Uhlenhake stood in the Cleveland Stadium locker room Sunday, shaking his head and saying, "We just lost the greatest quarterback in the NFL, maybe the greatest ever," and this was so true. The loss is football's, sports', not just ours. To lose Marino now would not be a far cry from losing Michael Jordan, except that Michael chose his time. Michael had his choice.

Marino will be back, certainly. But the question in my mind will not go away. The question is big but comes in a whisper: Have we seen the last of Marino at the peak of his game? And has the quarterback himself seen his best chance for his Super Bowl dream scissored by scalpels?

The question had been put to Dan, delicately, if that was possible, in an emptying dressing room Sunday. "I'd rather not answer that," he said.

But he did. He always does. Marino stands in. He does not duck. When his passes sail and are intercepted, he answers.

When his season and maybe his last shot at winning The Ring snap in an instant, he answers.

"Obviously the question crosses your mind," he said.

If it crossed your mind and left, that would be fine. But questions like that hang around, ferment.

Whether he will ever again be the same Dan Marino and whether he will ever again have the championship shot that this season presented – darned straight those are questions Dan Marino deals with today.

He is 32, and that four-to-six-month rehab may be optimistic, a best-case scenario. A more common medical opinion is a six-month minimum. Dan Marino was a man wrenched out of his element Monday, a mere mortal, one more hospital patient lying still under the hot lights. "Marino Magic" would make no appearance at Imperial Point Medical Center in Fort Lauderdale. Football miracles were Danny Boy's private cottage industry, but a medical miracle... did not happen.

Marino had such an aura of invincibility built up over a record 145 consecutive starts, you half expected Shula to smile into the bank of microphones and say, "Well, it's good news on Marino. They found the Achilles' tendon was just stretched. He should be back in a couple weeks."

Marino lay powerless, no football in sight, as team doctors Peter Indelicato and Dan Kanell worked scalpels behind his right foot for just under an hour early Monday afternoon. The operation went great – but it was still awful news for the Dolphins and their fans.

His right leg will be in a cast one to two months, during which time the muscles will atrophy. His right leg will become smaller than the left, requiring a rebuilding of strength. He will be confined to very limited range of motion while in the cast, after which rehabilitation will gradually begin.

All the while Marino will stay active in team meetings and on the sideline. But it may be next summer before he is able to drop back and plant and throw with any confidence.

Marino Injured

A concerned Don Shula leads the way as Marino is helped off the field with a ruptured Achilles tendon.

Fearful teammates gather around an injured Dan Marino.

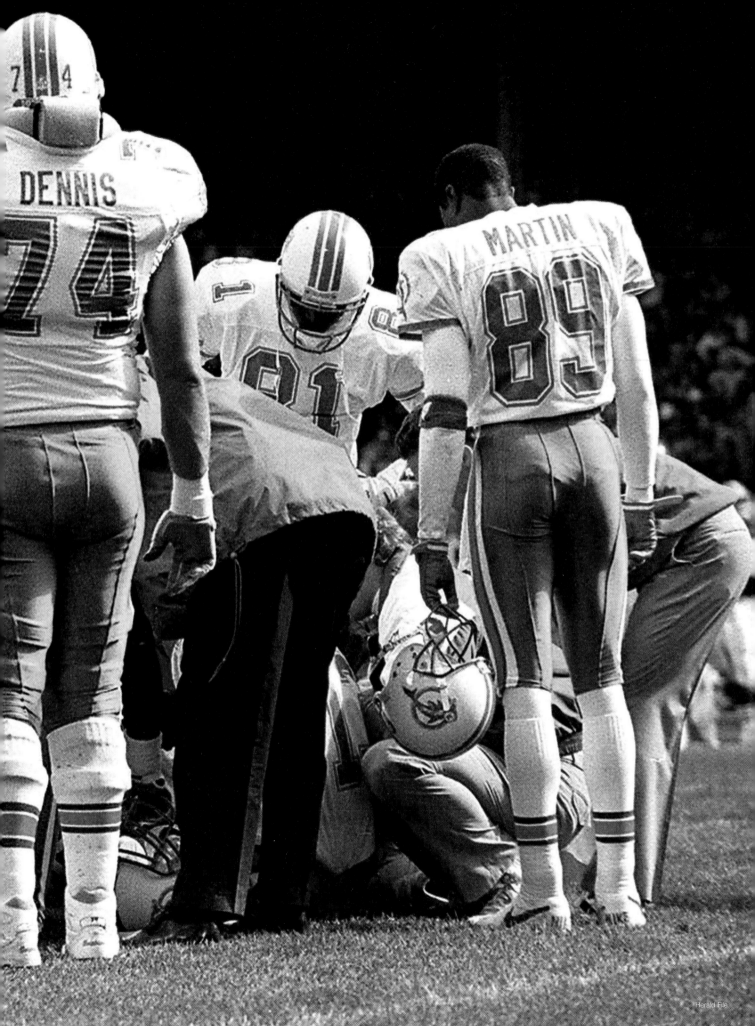

Herald File

Not knowing the full extent of the injury, Marino is examined on Dolphin bench.

Others have come back from Achilles' tears; Giants line-backer Lawrence Taylor did. But humans heal differently. Surgeons don't give guarantees.

Marino was said to be groggy and unavailable to be interviewed Monday. He went home soon after the surgery. His doctors were leaving all statements to Shula.

The coach said scrutiny of game film determined Marino was injured on a play so routine, so ordinary.

"It happened as he went back on his normal backpedal and planted with the weight on the ball of his foot," Shula said. "Something he's probably done a million times..."

Marino and heir–to–the–air Scott Mitchell spoke after the game.

"He said, 'It's been a long run. I've been healthy for a long time,'" Mitchell recalled. "It was obvious he was down."

The parallel to 1972 is such a weird coincidence, it demands mention. It was in Game 5 that year when Bob Griese went down, and Earl Morrall stepped in, and the victories kept coming. Similarities stop there. Morrall was a veteran, not inexperienced like Mitchell. Morrall had Larry Csonka and Mercury Morris to make him look very good. And Griese, for all of his accomplishment, was no Marino.

It may be tougher for Scott Mitchell to step in, to step up.

It may be tougher still for Dan Marino to hang in, to believe... to some day be Dan Marino again. ■

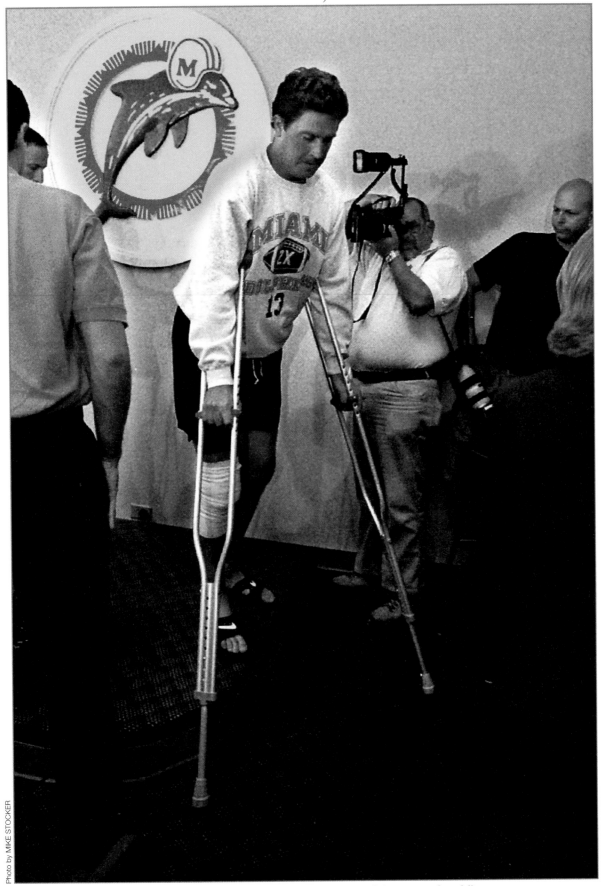

Photo by MIKE STOCKER

Marino leaves a press conference after discussing his surgery and the prognosis for a full recovery.

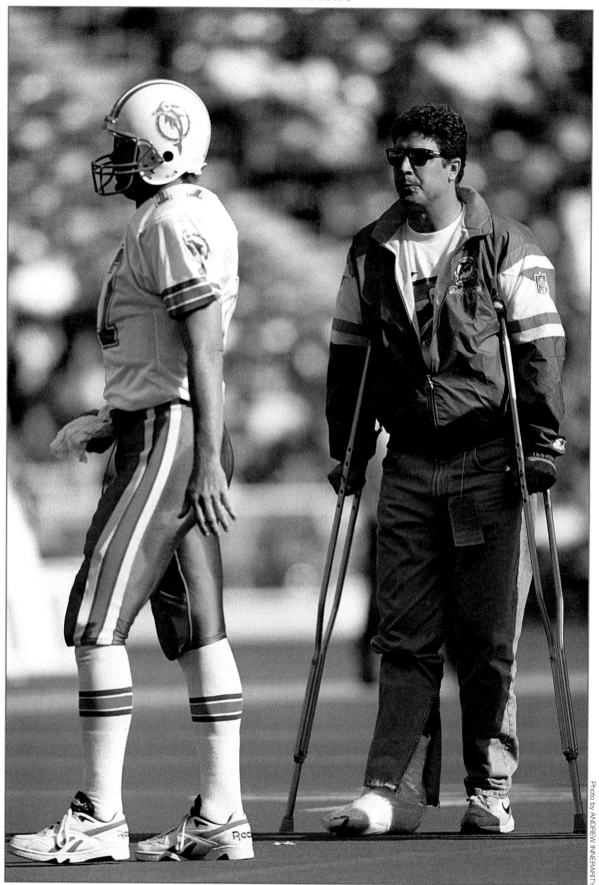

Marino watches as replacement quarterback Steve De Berg leaves the field.

Photo by ANDREW INNERARITY

Photo by WALTER MICHOT

Wearing the familiar brace on his left leg, Marino works on his comeback from Achilles tendon surgery on is right leg.

Marino Returns From Injury

By Armando Salguero

Monday, September 5, 1994

It could be said the Dolphins have the amnesia offense. It makes you forget about the problems on defense. That is exactly what happened Sunday after the Dolphins beat the New England Patriots, 39–35, in a heart–stopping, nail–biting affair that would please any offensive coordinator. The Dolphins were breaking offensive records in bunches as Dan Marino proved that a week's worth of talk about his uncertain status isn't worth the newspaper or radio waves it comes in. In a shootout with New England quarterback Drew Bledsoe, Marino emerged with the higher–caliber arm, riddling the Patriots for 473 yards and five touchdown passes.

Not that Bledsoe was shooting blanks. The second–year quarterback turned the Patriots' conservative offense into a mirror–image of Miami's pass–happy group, completing 32 of 51 passes for 421 yards and four touchdowns – the highest yardage total ever for a Patriots QB.

"There were nine touchdown passes out there, and fortunately we had five of them," Dolphins Coach Don Shula said. "I would have been devastated if we had lost it. The defense struggled, but when we had to have the win, they held."

The Miami defense held the lead on New England's final two possessions, and those two successful series erased the sins of five previous New England scoring drives.

"When you come out of a game like this, you don't say the offense played well and we didn't, so we should feel bad," linebacker Bryan Cox said. "The offense bailed us out, but we did what we had to do at the end of the game to win. We won, and that's the only thing that counts. Everything else isn't important."

It was important that Marino returned to his former self, and he seemed to play better than he has the past couple of years. Miami burned the New England defense as Marino accounted for seven NFL and/or Dolphins records and played a part in six others.

A SYNOPSIS OF THE RECORDS:

• Marino's five touchdown passes broke the NFL record he shared with Johnny Unitas for career games with four or more touchdown passes. The new record is 18.

• The 473 yards passing was the second–highest Dolphins total behind his own record of 521 yards set against the Jets in 1988. The total was also the highest produced by a Miami quarterback on opening day, breaking the record of 327 yards by Bob Griese in 1969.

• The game was Marino's first five–TD game since 1988.

• Marino joined Fran Tarkenton as the only players to throw 300 career touchdowns. Marino did it with his second TD pass.

"Dan's back," Shula proclaimed during his postgame press conference, alluding to Marino's first action since the October game in which he suffered a ruptured right Achilles' tendon.

"I felt pretty good about what I did," said Marino, who even brought the Joe Robbie Stadium crowd of 69,613 to its feet with a 10–yard run at the end of the first quarter. "I moved OK. It doesn't feel like it did in the past, but it's good enough."

Irving Fryar was the primary beneficiary of Marino's

Photo by DAVID BERGMAN

Marino celebrates a touchdown pass in his first game back from Achilles tendon surgery

*Wide receiver Irving
Fryar burns New
England's defense.*

"It would have been a 52–yard field goal, and if we had missed it, that might have been the ballgame," Shula said. "I wanted to take our shot."

New England cornerback Rod Smith must have felt the shot right through his heart. He was the defender asked to cover Fryar man–to–man on the play.

"It was a do–or–die situation, and I had man coverage," Fryar said. "Dan has played in the league long enough to recognize who had the man coverage, and he went to me. I just thank God we were able to get it done."

The Miami offensive players must have been saying a little prayer on New England's final two drives, on which their defensive mates were asked to do something they hadn't been able to manage most of the day – stop the Patriots.

It didn't look like that would happen right away, however, because Bledsoe found tight end Ben Coates on a 23–yard completion down the New England sideline on the first of those two possessions. But as Coates was rumbling to the Dolphins' 30, safety Gene Atkins popped him to dislodge the football.

Coates finished with eight receptions for 161 yards and two touchdowns; the fumble was only the second of his four–year career. But those facts were little consolation when the ball was recovered near the sideline by Dolphins strong safety Michael Stewart.

"I thank God the ball just laid their without going out of bounds," Stewart said.

"I don't know who knocked it out," Coates said. "It shouldn't have come out, but it did. I don't know what to say."

The Patriots had another chance at victory with 1:18 to play, but again the Miami defense rose to the challenge.

With a first down at midfield, Bledsoe threw four consecutive incomplete passes. The shootout was over. The Dolphins had won.

"This was the first game of the season, and anything goes," linebacker Chris Singleton said. "We never got frustrated, we never got our hopes dashed. Our offense scored a lot of points, and the defense stopped them when it counted. That's all anybody cares about in here." ■

aerials, and he, too, had a record–setting day.

Fryar caught five passes for 211 yards and three scores, setting a personal high for yards.

"It's been a long time for me since I've had such a good game catching the ball," Fryar said. "I've had better games blocking and carrying out some other assignments, but I can't remember gaining so much yardage."

Marino completed passes to seven different receivers. Even Scott Miller – who caught three passes for 55 yards – set career highs for receptions and yards.

Fryar's three touchdown catches were spectacular. He had a 54–yarder, a 50–yarder off a flea–flicker and a 35–yarder that was the difference in the game.

That final catch came on fourth and five with 3:19 left to play. Shula elected to go for the first down rather than the field goal, partly because the attempt would have come from the treacherous baseball infield and partly because it would have been a long kick.

Photo by DAVID BERGMAN

Back in familiar form, Marino looks down-field.

*O. J. McDuffie rumbles
downfield against the Patriots.*

Photo by DAVID BERGMAN

The Clock Play

By Bob Rubin

November 28, 1994

"Clock! Clock! Clock!" was actually a "Crock! Crock! Crock!" Forget the quarterback sneak. The Dolphins have the sneak quarterback.

What a fake. What a ruse. What a scam.

What a gas.

How deceptive. How underhanded. How wicked.

How delightful.

Dan Marino gets four stars for his passing and his acting in Sunday's magnificent, had-to-have-it comeback victory over the Jets. His first three touchdowns passes were routinely brilliant (or brilliantly routine) Marino, but it's the fourth, the eight-yarder to Mark Ingram with 22 seconds to play to win the game, we will remember merely forever.

For you hard-core football types, its name in the playbook is Fake Spike Pretend to Kill the Clock Lull Opponents to Sleep Throw a Game-Winning Touchdown Pass Curl Cross Hook Zig Zag In Out Boop Boop Be Doop. On two.

In keeping with the spirit of the play, I lied. It's actually called "Clock."

Marino has acted before. He appeared in a movie, *Ace Ventura: Pet Detective*. He hawks gloves and cars in TV ads. But this was his crowning moment as a thespian.

"I am," he said Monday with a credible attempt at dignity, "an accomplished actor."

He certainly was on "Clock." Bernie Kosar, who brought the play with him from Cleveland, suggested it over the radio headset as Marino was jogging toward the line of scrimmage after his completion to the eight.

Marino had already thought of it. Both veteran quarterbacks were aware the Jets had a rookie, Aaron Glenn, at left cornerback. Both thought: "Pigeon."

The Dolphins had tried "Clock" against the Vikings Sept. 25. One lineman did

Marino's preferred target Mark Ingram awaits the surprise touchdown pass...

Photo by JOE RIMKUS JR.

...and rejoices after catching the Jets off guard.

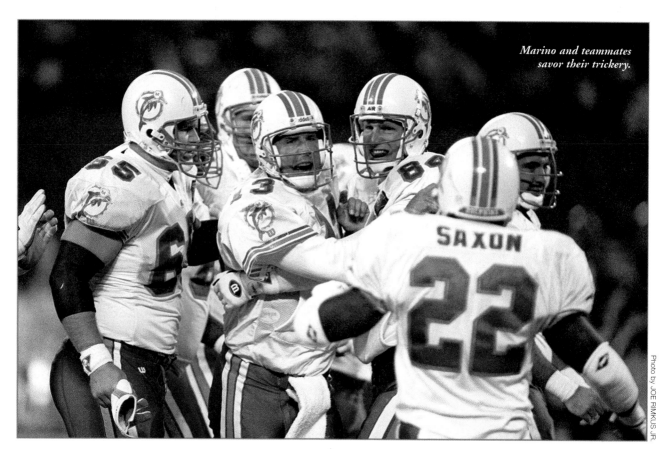

Marino and teammates savor their trickery.

Photo by JOE RIMKUS JR.

not block and a Viking broke through, forcing Marino to throw the ball away.

But that wasn't a problem against the Jets. They were so taken in by Marino and teammates screaming "Clock! Clock! Clock!" and pointing at the ground with their palms down, they just stood around when the ball was snapped, sure Marino was going to spike it.

Both wideouts take off on "Clock." So focused was Marino on Ingram, who was covered by Glenn, he couldn't remember who was on the other side.

The picture that appeared on the front page of The Herald sports section Monday says it all about how badly bamboozled was poor Glenn. Ingram is turning around to catch the ball in the end zone while Glenn is running past him, looking straight ahead.

The Jets had been had. Big time.

They were stunned. Huh? What happened? Is that legal? Aw, fudge.

Smiling at the memory, center Jeff Dellenbach said, "One of them was yelling at the refs, 'Hey, they called clock! Where's the flag? Where's the flag?' Like if we

called it, we had to do it."

Ingram said Glenn had a two-word reaction.

"He used a four-letter word with Marino after it."

Some Jets players or fans may feel it's unethical and dishonorable to win in such a fashion. After much careful deliberation and serious soul searching, I offer the following response:

Nyah nyah nyah nyah nyah. ■

Wide receiver Mark Ingram welcomes the second of his three touchdown catches in the victory over the Jets.

The Comebacks

 By Jason Cole

Someday long from now, football historians will marvel at how Dan Marino made the comeback mundane. Not that Marino was any better than someone such as Joe Montana or John Elway in creating fourth-quarter heroic drives. It's just that Marino, who produced 36 fourth-quarter comebacks out of the 164 total games the Dolphins won in his career, operated with a precision that few others could master.

Marino's inability to scramble – unlike Montana and Elway – meant he had to do almost all his work from the pocket. There were almost no scrambles on third-and-8, no improvised pass routes as he scrambled to his right and a receiver came back to him.

Marino was so good at throwing the ball, he could do it when he was semiconscious.

On Sept. 27, 1992, at Seattle, Marino was knocked loopy by a Seahawks defensive lineman on the Dolphins' final drive. He was helped off the field and missed a play. He came back on the next play, still wobbly with a concussion, and threw the game-winning touchdown pass.

After the game, Marino couldn't remember the play.

Teammates agree Marino made Miami's offense unique.

"It was different than other places I played," said Ron Heller, an offensive tackle with the Dolphins from 1993 to 1995. "When I was in Philadelphia [with quarterback Randall Cunningham], it would be something crazy that would happen. Randall would scramble for awhile and then the play would break down and somebody would get open."

"With Dan, it was just like everything was the same as a normal drive, just a little faster," Heller said. "You can say it's ice water in his veins and all that stuff, but it's more. He's just so comfortable

Turning the tables on the Tennessee Oilers in a comeback victory in 1997.

Photo by PATRICK FARRELL

Photo by BILL FRAKES

Mark Duper celebrates a touchdown pass in a 20-16 comeback against the Jets.

Marino consoles Peyton Manning after beating the Colts 34-31.

Photo by JOE RIMKUS JR

under pressure. He knows exactly what he wants to do and he knows it faster than anybody."

A lot faster, actually.

"He had an amazing ability to be incredibly precise," Sports Illustrated NFL writer Paul Zimmerman said. "He could do more in 20 or 30 or 40 seconds than any quarterback I've ever seen."

A key element was Marino's ability to communicate with a nod or some other minor gesture. That would put him and his receivers on the same page.

For instance, there was the famous "Clock Play" in New York against the Jets on Nov. 27, 1994, when Marino led the Dolphins to a 28-24 victory. The Dolphins had been down 24-6 at one point in the third quarter. Marino and wide receiver Mark Ingram combined for four touchdowns, but the last one was the topper.

With the clock winding down in the final minute, the Dolphins reached the Jets' 8-yard line for a first-and-goal. The standard play at that point is to run the clock play, throwing the ball into the turf to stop the clock.

Marino was yelling for the clock play but telling Ingram something different with his eyes. In Marino's earpiece, backup quarterback Bernie Kosar was saying, "Go after the rookie," meaning Jets first-year cornerback Aaron

Glenn.

With the Jets expecting the ball to be downed, Marino instead fired a quick toss to Ingram for the winning touchdown with 22 seconds remaining. The Jets lost the game standing flat-footed and Marino showed uncommon joy by jumping around like a 12-year-old who had just hit his first Little League home run.

Ingram was asked how, in all the confusion and running around, did he know Marino was going to throw it to him.

"He just gave me a look," Ingram said.

Marino's communication to receivers without using words showed repeatedly.

In the 1994 season opener against New England, the Dolphins faced a critical fourth-and-5 play from the Patriots' 35-yard line late in the game. Coach Don Shula sent in tight end Keith Jackson with a safe, short-pass play.

But when the Patriots challenged the Dolphins, showing blitz and playing tight man coverage on the wide receivers, Marino audibled and hit wide receiver Irving Fryar for the winning score with 3:19 remaining.

What added to the aura of that game was that it was Marino's first after missing 11 games in 1993 with a torn Achilles' tendon. Marino finished with 473 yards and five touchdowns.

Marino capped his own personal comeback with another signature team comeback.

"He had the guts to call plays like that," said former New York Jets quarterback Ken O'Brien, who was drafted along with Marino in the first round of 1983, "he burned us, too. I was sitting there on the sideline watching. . . I started screaming at our defense, 'No, get back.' I saw Dan later and we just laughed about that." ■

Grace under pressure: Marino comes back to beat the Falcons 21-17.

*Keith Byars hauls in a Marino
TD pass to tie the game against
the Raiders. Dolphins go on to
win in overtime 20-17*

Dandy Victory

 By Edwin Pope

Sunday, January 1, 1995

On the Dolphins' sideline with the clock running out and thunder coming down from the stands, Dan Marino wore a baseball cap. He looked like you imagine Sandy Koufax might have in a football helmet.

Marino danced on one leg and wiped humidity-greasy palms on a towel slung around his shoulder. His eyes never left the Joe Robbie Stadium field where old Joe Montana grappled with the Dolphins with no timeouts left.

The Kansas City Chiefs died with 15 seconds left on the clock, 15 seconds they will never use, and Marino ran back out and knelt and officially ended a victory for which he had waited 10 long, long years.

Marino threw one look at the score, MIAMI 27, K.C. 17, on the JumboTRON. Then his bright, glistening eyes began searching the gathering mob for Montana. He finally found him, and they came together about as well as anyone can in the middle of such madness.

"Joe and I didn't really say anything," Marino said. "There were too many people there."

For a while Saturday night, it seemed there were too few Dolphins there every time Montana took a snap.

"I felt like I had to score every time we got the ball," Marino said, half-laughing.

Montana, the 38-year-old legend, was not even half-laughing after he and the Chiefs fell to Marino's blazing hand and two titanic takeaways by J.B. Brown and Michael Stewart.

If Marino's second half was restrained by comparison to his first, at least his drive opening the third quarter was masterpiece stuff.

At one point, he was hurrying the Dolphins to line up so fast the Chiefs had to burn a timeout to get themselves together. Then he threw over a blitz on the seven-yard touchdown to Irving Fryar that put the Dolphins ahead, 24-17. Ahead for good.

What started as perpetual Montana turned into perpetual Marino. There has never been a better one. Marino has posted bigger numbers, but never more artfully.

In this first round of National Football League playoffs, he was unleashing controlled rockets. Not once did he heave the desperate bomb that marked so many frustrating years before he went down for the last 11 games of last season.

"This is a great feeling after being hurt like that," Marino said.

He stood uncomfortably at a lectern, which he hates, "because I want to be treated like all the other guys." He answered questions almost by rote.

Did he settle a score with Montana, who had crushed him – but not humbled him – in that 38-16 runaway in the 19th Super Bowl 10 years ago?

"There was no score to settle," Marino said. "I've said all week Joe is incredible, and has had a great career."

But there was a score to settle. There always will be, until Marino gets back to and wins at least one Super Bowl.

The Dolphins might get that chance if Marino puts on two more shows like Saturday's.

He finished with two touchdown passes, that seven-yarder to Fryar and a yard's worth to Ronnie Williams, who was open enough for you and me to hit him.

Marino completed 22 of 29 passes for 257 yards without an interception, while Montana was going 26 for 37 for 314 yards, with that one huge interception by J.B. Brown. Marino could have been perfect except for drops.

Trying to get him to articulate his magic is, of course, futile. It is like asking Koufax to explain a pitch, Rubinstein a stroke of piano keys, Michael Jordan hanging in the air beside a basket as though he is never coming down.

Photo by DAVID BERGMAN

Marino takes charge against Joe Montana and the Chiefs.

A young fan's sign says it all.

Photo by JOE RINKUS JR.

has had to fire almost when the snap hit his hand. But he never complains about the blockers. They are his lifeline, and Saturday all of them – Heller, Richmond Webb, Keith Sims, Bert Weidner, Jeff Dellenbach – did their parts and more.

In the end, though, Marino made it work. There are blessed days in all the lives of the luckiest of us when everything we touch turns strawberry, and this was one of those for Marino.

"He was great today," Chiefs cornerback Mark Collins said. "He read all our checks. I don't think we could have done anything more defensively than we did, except maybe get an interception."

Smith, the man Heller had to block, said, "Marino was big on third down." Smith rolled his eyes. "And a lot of other times, too."

That pretty much sums up 10 years for Miamarino, when he has had so many great Septembers and so many fewer bright Januarys than he deserves. He isn't the only QB in the universe, but who else could have given us so much and still left us just as thirsty for what he may yet bring? ■

None of this is something you can learn. Marino just knows, as Montana knows. And if Montana seemed to know exactly where every man on both teams was on every play at the very beginning, Marino got the idea soon enough. He was throwing underneath to his backs, and when the Chiefs came up to stop that, he started hitting his wide receivers and tight ends.

When Marino is on and his offensive line is close enough to perfect to not only knock people off Danny Boy but out of the way for his runners, no one can stop him.

He did not have quite those kinds of linemen or runners when Montana and the 49ers blasted the Dolphins back in Palo Alto, Jan. 20, 1985. He will never say that, but he was acknowledging it Saturday night when he saluted tackle Ron Heller in particular.

"Ron was hurt and going against an All-Pro (Neil Smith)," Marino said. "And he did a hell of a job. Most games, I have a lot of time, but I had more than usual this time."

That is not strictly correct. In some games this kaleidoscopic season, Marino has been under such pressure he

"I felt like I had to score every time we got the ball" – Dan Marino on the victory against Montana.

Marino and Montana meet after the game…on the field together for the last time.

Marino And The Records

DOLPHINS RECORD WHEN MARINO...

Threw 0 Touchdowns...16-23
Was Not Intercepted...62-23
Threw 1 Touchdown..45-31
Was Intercepted...85-72
Threw 2 Touchdowns...45-20
Played on Grass...108-54
Threw 3 Touchdowns...25-16
Played on Turf..39-41
Threw 4 Touchdowns...12-3
Played in Domes..15-14
Threw 5 Touchdowns...4-1
Played on Monday Night..19-18
Threw 6 Touchdowns...0-1
Played on Sunday Night..11-4
Threw at least 1 TD..131-72
Played on Thursday Night...1-0
Was Not Sacked...68-33
Played in Prime Time...31-22
Was Sacked...79-62
Played in Overtime...7-8
Rushed for a Touchdown...7-2

MOST ALL-TIME VICTORIES BY NFL STARTING QUARTERBACKS

PLAYER	TEAMS	SEASONS	W-L-T	PCT
1. John Elway	Denver	16	148-82-1	.643
2. DAN MARINO	MIAMI	17	147-93-0	.613
3. Brett Favre	Green Bay	14	136-72-0	.654

NFL CAREER PASSING YARDAGE LEADERS
Note: ( ) - number of years played: * - active players

1. DAN MARINO 61,361 (17)
2. John Elway 51,475 (16)
3. Brett Favre* 49,734 (14)
4. Warren Moon 49,325 (17)
5. Fran Tarkenton 47,003 (18)
6. Vinny Testaverde* 44,475 (18)
7. Dan Fouts 43,040 (15)
8. Joe Montana 40,551 (16)
9. Johnny Unitas 40,239 (18)
10. Drew Bledsoe* 39,808 (12)
11. Dave Krieg 38,151 (19)
12. Boomer Esiason 37,920 (14)
13. Jim Kelly 35,467 (11)
14. Jim Everett 34,837 (12)
15. Jim Hart 34,665 (18)
16. Steve DeBerg 34,241 (17)
17. John Hadl 33,503 (16)
18. Phil Simms 33,462 (14)
19. Steve Young 33,124 (15)
20. Troy Aikman 32,942 (12)

Photo by DAVID BERGMAN

Acknowledging a standing ovation after breaking Fran Tarkenton's record for all-time passing yards.

Marino accepts congratulations from former record-holder Fran Tarkenton.

TOP TWENTY, CAREER TOUCHDOWN PASSES
Note: ( ) - number of years played; * - active players

1. DAN MARINO 420 (17)
2. Brett Favre* 376 (14)
3. Fran Tarkenton 342 (18)
4. John Elway 300 (16)
5. Warren Moon 291 (17)
6. Johnny Unitas 290 (18)
7. Joe Montana 273 (16)
8. Vinny Testaverde* 268 (18)
9. Dave Krieg 261 (19)
10. Sonny Jurgensen 255 (18)
11. Dan Fouts 254 (15)
12. Boomer Esiason 247 (14)
13. John Hadl 244 (16)
14. Len Dawson 239 (19)
15. Jim Kelly 237 (11)
16. George Blanda 236 (26)
17. Steve Young 232 (15)
18. John Brodie 214 (16)
19. Y.A. Tittle 212 (15)
20. Terry Bradshaw 212 (14)

ALL-TIME NFL TOTAL OFFENSE LEADERS

Name	Seasons	Total Yards	Passing Yards	Rushing Yards
DAN MARINO	17	61,448	61,361	87
John Elway	16	54,882	51,475	3,407
Brett Favre	14	51,417	49,734	1,683
Warren Moon	17	51,061	49,325	1,736
Fran Tarkenton	18	50,677	47,003	3,674

ALL-TIME FOURTH QUARTER COMEBACK DRIVES

PLAYER	TEAMS	COMEBACK DRIVES
1. John Elway	Denver	43
2. DAN MARINO	MIAMI	37
3. Joe Montana	San Francisco	31
4. Jim Kelly	Buffalo	24

DOLPHINS STARTING QUARTERBACKS UNDER DON SHULA

QUARTERBACK	YEAR	STARTS
Bob Griese	1970-80	119
George Mira	1971	1
Earl Morrall	1972-76	12
Don Strock	1974-87	20
David Woodley	1980-83	40
DAN MARINO	1983-95	184
Kyle Mackey (Repl.)	1987	3
Scott Mitchell	1990-93	7
Steve DeBerg	1993	4
Bernie Kosar	1995	2

DON SHULA'S CAREER RECORD BY QUARTERBACK

Player	Regular Season	Playoffs	Overall Record
DAN MARINO	116-68-0 .630	6-07-0 .462	122-75-0 .619
Bob Griese	82-36-1 .693	6-05-0 .545	88-41-1 .681
David Woodley	27-12-1 .688	3-02-0 .600	30-14-1 .677
Don Strock	14-06-0 .600		14-06-0 .700
Earl Morrall	11-01-0 .917	2-00-0 1.000	13-01-0 .929
Scott Mitchell	3-04-0 .429		3-04-0 .429
Steve DeBerg	2-02-0 .500		2-02-0 .500
George Mira	1-00-0 1.000		1-00-0 1.000
Kyle Mackey	1-02-0 .333		1-02-0 .333
Bernie Kosar	0-02-0 .000		0-02-0 .000
TOTALS	257-133-2 .658	17-14-0 .548	274-147-2 .648

LONGEST RUNNING QB-COACH COMBINATIONS IN NFL HISTORY

QUARTERBACK	COACH	TEAM	YEARS TOGETHER
Terry Bradshaw	Chuck Noll	Pittsburgh	1970-1983 (14)
DAN MARINO	DON SHULA	MIAMI	1983-1995 (13)
Danny White	Tom Landry	Dallas	1976-1988 (13)
Len Dawson	Hank Stram	Kansas City	1963-1974 (12)
Bob Griese	Don Shula	Miami	1970-1980 (11)
Roger Staubach	Tom Landry	Dallas	1969-1979 (11)

MARINO'S MIAMI DOLPHINS CAREER PLAYOFF RECORDS

TD	Passes	Yards	Attempts	Completions	Interceptions
Marino	32	4,510	687	385	24
Griese	10	1,467	208	112	12

MOST PASSING YARDS IN NFL POSTSEASON HISTORY

PLAYER	TEAMS	YARDS	GAMES
Joe Montana	San Francisco/Kansas City	5,772	23
John Elway	Denver	4,964	22
Brett Favre	Green Bay	4,902	20
DAN MARINO	MIAMI	4,510	18
Jim Kelly	Buffalo	3,863	17

MOST TOUCHDOWN PASSES IN NFL POSTSEASON HISTORY

PLAYER	TEAMS	PASSES	GAMES
Joe Montana	San Francisco/Kansas City	45	23
Brett Favre	Green Bay	33	19
DAN MARINO	MIAMI	32	18
Terry Bradshaw	Pittsburgh	30	19
John Elway	Denver	27	22

Photo by DAVID BERGMAN

Don Shula puts his arm around the new record holder,

97

NFL RECORD, TOUCHDOWN PASSES IN CONSECUTIVE PLAYOFF GAMES

PLAYER	TEAM	SEASONS	GAMES WITH A TD PASS
Brett Favre	Green Bay	1995-04	(current) 16
DAN MARINO	MIAMI	1983-95	13
Joe Montana	San Francisco	1988-90	10
Ken Stabler	Oakland	1973-77	10
John Elway	Denver	1984-89	09

YOUNGEST PRO BOWL QUARTERBACKS (1970-02)

Note: * Did not play due to injury: # Named to squad by AFC coaching staff as a "need" player

QUARTERBACK	TEAM	YEAR	AGE
DAN MARINO*	MIAMI	1983	22 YEARS, 4 MONTHS, 14 DAYS
Michael Vick	Atlanta	2002	22 years, 7 months, 7 days
Drew Bledsoe	New England	1994	22 years, 11 months, 22 days
Brett Favre	Green Bay	1992	23 years, 3 months, 28 days
DAN MARINO	MIAMI	1984	23 YEARS, 4 MONTHS, 12 DAYS
Peyton Manning	Indianapolis	1999	23 years, 10 months, 6 days
Bernie Kosar#	Cleveland	1987	24 years, 2 months, 13 days

DAN MARINO'S NFL REGULAR SEASON STATISTICS

YEAR	TEAM	G-S	ATT.	COMP.	YDS.	PCT.	TD	INT.	LG	TKLD.	RATE
1983	Miami	11-9	296	173	2210	58.4	20	6	85t	10/80	96.0
1984	Miami	16-16	564	362	5084	64.2	48	17	80t	13/120	108.9
1985	Miami	16-16	567	336	4137	59.3	30	21	73t	18/157	84.1
1986	Miami	16-16	623	378	4746	60.7	44	23	85t	17/119	92.5
1987	Miami	12-12	444	263	3245	59.2	26	13	59t	9/77	89.2
1988	Miami	16-16	606	354	4434	58.4	28	23	80t	6/31	80.8
1989	Miami	16-16	550	308	3997	56.0	24	22	78t	10/86	76.9
1990	Miami	16-16	531	306	3563	57.6	21	11	69t	15/90	82.6
1991	Miami	16-16	549	318	3970	57.9	25	13	54t	27/182	85.8
1992	Miami	16-16	554	330	4116	59.6	24	16	62t	28/173	85.1
1993	Miami	5-5	150	91	1218	60.7	8	3	80t	7/42	95.9
1994	Miami	16-16	615	385	4453	62.6	30	17	64t	17/113	89.2
1995	Miami	14-14	482	309	3668	64.1	24	15	67t	22/153	90.8
1996	Miami	13-13	373	221	2795	59.2	17	9	74t	18/131	87.8
1997	Miami	16-16	548	319	3780	58.2	16	11	55	20/142	80.7
1998	Miami	16-16	537	310	3497	57.7	23	15	61t	23/178	80.0
1999	Miami	11-11	369	204	2448	55.3	12	17	62	9/66	67.4
17-YEAR TOTALS		**242-240**	**8358**	**4967**	**61361**	**59.4**	**420**	**252**	**85t**	**269/1940**	**86.4**

DAN MARINO'S NFL PLAYOFF STATISTICS

YEAR	TEAM	G-S	ATT.	COMP	YDS.	PCT.	TD	INT.	LG	TKLD.	RATE
1983	Miami	1-1	25	15	193	60.0	2	2	32t	0/0	77.6
1984	Miami	3-3	116	71	1001	61.2	8	5	41t	4/29	94.1
1985	Miami	2-2	93	45	486	48.4	3	3	39t	1/14	61.5
1990	Miami	2-2	79	42	544	53.2	5	2	64t	2/8	85.6
1992	Miami	2-2	74	39	435	52.7	4	2	30t	4/25	77.3
1994	Miami	2-2	67	46	519	68.7	5	0	31t	2/13	116.4
1995	Miami	1-1	64	33	422	51.6	2	3	45t	0/0	63.4
1997	Miami	1-1	43	17	141	39.5	0	2	42	4/21	29.3
1998	Miami	2-2	71	49	478	69.0	1	3	56	2/12	74.7
1999	Miami	2-2	55	28	291	50.9	2	2	27	3/19	63.5
PLAYOFF TOTALS		**18-18**	**687**	**385**	**4510**	**56.0**	**32**	**24**	**64t**	**22/141**	**77.1**

MARINO'S NFL RECORDS

Most Attempts, Career 8,358

Most Completions, Career 4,967

Most Yards Passing, Career 61,361

Most Touchdown Passes, Career..420

Highest Pass Rating, Rookie Season ....96.0 in 1983

Highest Completion Percentage, Rookie Season............58.45 in 1983 (296-173)

Most Yards Gained, Season ....5,084 in 1984

Most Games, 400 or more Yards Passing, Career...13

Most Games, 300 or more Yards Passing, Career...60

Most Seasons, 3,000 or more Yards Passing 13 (1984-92, 1994-95, 1997-98)

Most Games, Four or more Touchdown Passes, Career....................................21

Lowest Percentage, Passes Had Intercepted, Rookie Season..2.03 in 1983 (296-6)

Most Seasons Leading League, Attempts 5 (1984, 1986, 1988, 1992, 1997)

Most Seasons Leading League, Completions 6 (1984-86, 1988, 1992, 1997)

Most Seasons, 40 or more Touchdown Passes.................................2 (1984, 1986)

Most Seasons, 20 or more Touchdown Passes...........13 (1983-92, 1994-95, 1998)

100 TD Passes in Fewest Amount of Games to Start Career.........44 (9/7/86 at S.D.)

200 TD passes in Fewest Amount of Games to Start Career.......89 (9/17/89 at N.E.)

300 TD passes in Fewest Amount of Games to Start Career......157 (9/4/94 vs. N.E.)

(left) The Marino records exhibit in Canton, Ohio.
(above)"Dan the Man"

Photo by JOE RIMKUS JR

Photo by DAVID BERGMAN

The Last Big Win

 By Edwin Pope

Monday, January 10, 2000
SEATTLE

Network cameras frantically chased Jimmy Johnson in the deathly silence of a Kingdome doomed to be blown to bits soon. The Dolphins head coach wheeled away from them, scanning the field for Dan Marino.

"Dan! Dan!" Johnson bellowed. Then J.J. thrust his right thumb triumphantly into the air.

Together Marino and Johnson – and a whole passel of other Dolphins – had blown the Seahawks out of the postseason, 20-17, in the Kingdome's last game before it's exploded to make room for a new football house.

Together Marino and Johnson had knocked off the monkey that had ridden the Dolphins' back for 27 years, and created a second postseason step against Jacksonville's Jaguars up there Saturday. As every South Florida schoolchild must know by now, the Dolphins – before Sunday – hadn't won a postseason game on the road since 1972.

I don't believe Miamarino ever even heard or saw Johnson yell for him in the chaos at game's end. Marino was trotting through battalions of photographers, holding tightly to the football that would be designated as the "game ball" and presented to the warrior who made what was truly, for the Dolphins, a miracle.

He passed for 84 yards on the Dolphins' 85-yard drive to the winning touchdown. That was some three times as much as the 28 yards he had produced in the first half when the Dolphins were playing it cozy, strictly by the coach's plan to run the ball and avoid turnovers.

The Seahawks had led all the way when Marino lined up his offense at Miami's 15 with 9:09 left. Yet, even in this head-hammering din, you never got the idea the Seahawks were in command.

Two plays later, Marino faced third and 17 at his 8. This really isn't where an offense wants to be, down 17-13 and trying to hold itself together in the incredible noise generated by 66,170 fans who sound more like six million.

"We ran a square-in (where the receiver runs a few yards downfield and then directly laterally)," Marino said, "and Tony Martin made a great catch."

Twenty-three yards' worth of great.

You know the funniest thing of all (if you don't live in Seattle)?

"The Seahawks called a timeout before the play and still couldn't get in the right defense," one Dolphins coach said.

MAGIC OF THE PAST

Remorselessly, as in days of yore, 38-year-old Marino visited one horror after another on the panicked Seahawks. He hit Martin twice more for 17 and 20 yards, and the underrated Oronde Gadsden for 24 before J.J. Johnson ran the final two yards and the stadium went as quiet as the biggest tomb you ever saw.

Someone asked Marino if he had been thinking about all the will-he-retire-or-won't-he talk when he got hot in the fourth quarter.

"I'm not that smart, to think about all that stuff at once," Marino said. "Especially with all that noise. This is about as loud as it gets."

So, for now, the questions of whether either Marino or Johnson or both will retire from the Dolphins go on hold. The only thing really important for now is the Jagville game, and how much better a chance the Dolphins have today than they would have had in the last couple of months of the regular season when they lost six of their last eight games.

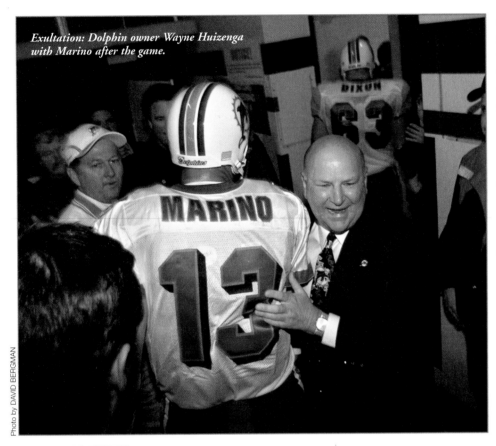

Exultation: Dolphin owner Wayne Huizenga with Marino after the game.

Photo by DAVID BERGMAN

quarter, the Dolphins ran on a third and six and passed on a third and one, and neither worked. The first play was to put the Seahawks on notice that they would have to stop the Dolphins' running game, even in passing situations. The second play just didn't work.

But between the offense and a defense that harried 'Hawks all afternoon, the job got done.

STILL IN THE HUNT

It got done because the coaches saw that the best players got the ball in critical situations, and the best defenders - like Trace Armstrong with his three sacks - were in position to make 'Hawk-killing plays.

Marino turned terrific when he had to. Martin's one-handed pull-in of that 23-yarder on third and 17 was his best catch all year. Armstrong, Zach Thomas and Rich Owens hit their stride when it mattered most.

Until next Saturday.

At least, though, the Dolphins have a chance at the big one. For once, they aren't going home in disgrace. For once in his 17 seasons, Marino wore a postseason grin the size of a slice of watermelon.

"Heck yeah, I'm excited," he said.

For Marino, that's a speech.

He had already delivered a more telling one, with third and 17 from his 8-yard line, in the Dolphins' biggest postseason play since four years before the Kingdome was even built. And now they're blowing up the joint. Just like the Dolphins did the Seahawks. ■

TEAM WAS READY

Racing off the field, Johnson grabbed my ear and shouted into it, "Didn't I tell you we'd be prepared?"

He did exactly that, just the other morning. He talked about how upbeat he was. He talked about how, if you properly deal with one play at a time, the game will take care of itself.

"I told the players all week it's not the bad things that happen that make you lose," he said Sunday night. "It's how you react. It's about confidence and not letting it break. You let it break, you lose one game, and then it's two and three and four before you know it."

J.J. and his staff and the Dolphins saw to it that not many bad things even threatened their confidence. They collected two turnovers - interceptions by Brock Marion and Terrell Buckley - without ever turning the ball over themselves. They ran the ball 37 times and threw it only 30 times.

"[Offensive coordinator] Kippy Brown did a great job," Johnson said.

Some of the calls seemed a little strange. In the second

Why Wasn't J.J. At The Farewell? He Wasn't Welcome

By Armando Salguero

Wednesday, March 15, 2000

Jimmy Johnson is being unfairly convicted of a transgression he did not commit.

The former Dolphins coach was noticeable by his absence Monday when Dan Marino announced his NFL retirement at the Dolphins' training facility. Pundits aware of the strained relationship between Johnson and Marino immediately ripped Johnson for missing a dual opportunity to honor the quarterback and repair the relationship.

Except that Johnson agreed to attend when he was first told of the news conference. Johnson agreed his absence in the face of Dave Wannstedt's and Don Shula's presence would look dubious.

Johnson simply agreed to do the right thing.

But over the weekend, Johnson was told to stay away. In no uncertain terms.

You see, in directing the planning of his farewell just as he directed countless touchdown drives, Marino decided it would not be appropriate for Johnson to be present.

Marino would have felt uncomfortable.

That's exactly how Marino felt for much of the time he played under Johnson the past four years.

The two men had good times, sure, but also were often involved in tension-filled bouts that pitted their large egos and iron wills against each other.

Those bouts wore on both men. Johnson's friends say the Marino issue was one reason the coach retired. And Marino's friends say the quarterback, though publicly silent about the feud, often went home and did what millions of Americans do around their loved ones.

He complained about his boss.

"I can't begin to tell you some of the things Dan told me about how bad things got last season," former Buffalo quarterback and Marino confidant Jim Kelly

All smiles: Jimmy Johnson arrives as the Dolphins head coach in 1996.

Photo by JOE RIMKUS JR

"Jimmy" and "Danny" headed down what would become a bumpy road in this 1997 pre-season promotion.

Photo by DAVID BERGMAN

Marino gets an enthusiastic handshake from Johnson after throwing a touchdown in pre-season against the Bears.

Marino may not have felt he could be so brutally honest with Johnson in the audience. And if he had been, the media would have run to Johnson for reaction, then back to Marino for reaction to Johnson's reaction.

It would have spawned a circus – like situation and cast a shadow on Marino's final moments in the sun.

Even if Marino hadn't offered his honest assessment of his relationship with Johnson – a footnote on a day meant to honor his great body of work – Johnson's mere presence would have attenuated the spotlight on Marino.

That's because Johnson has not answered questions since Miami's 62-7 playoff loss to Jacksonville. So Johnson's next public appearance will feature a Keystone Kops–type media chase for that first juicy interview.

Marino's farewell news conference was not the right venue for that. Instead, Monday was Marino's day and his alone. Rightfully so.

Understand, the uncovering of these facts are not meant to protect Jimmy Johnson. Heaven knows there was plenty wrong with the way he left the Dolphins.

He did not win a championship like he promised.

He did not find a running game like he promised.

He did not leave the team with the $5 million to $6 million in salary cap room this offseason like he promised.

He is culpable of those failures. But of snubbing Dan Marino on the day of his retirement? Jimmy Johnson did no such thing. ∎

said when we talked briefly at the Super Bowl.

Marino wasn't wrong in not wanting Johnson around. It's simply how he felt and, frankly, it would have smacked of poorly veiled hypocrisy for the outgoing legend to betray his own feelings.

No photo opportunity is worth that.

Johnson's absence allowed Marino to speak his mind when the question everyone knew was coming finally arrived. Marino was asked if his time with Johnson was a difficult one.

"I would just have to say that our relationship was up and down at times," Marino said. "And coach Johnson, we had some great, great days together and some fun times. And sometimes I wasn't very happy here while he was coaching, and that's just being honest."

An anxious Johnson looks at the clock with Marino in the background in a 1997 game against Tennessee.

The cold relationship freezes over. Johnson watches replay of Marino's fourth interception against the Cowboys.

End of the road: Dan Marino surveys the field as time runs out on what proved to be his last game, a 62–7 playoff loss in Jacksonville to the Jaguars.

Dan Marino And The Community – No One Ever Gave More

 By Dan LeBatard

March 14, 2000

Dear Dolphins:

My son, Noah, was born with VATER Syndrome, which included no esophagus, radial dysplasia on both hands, no use of his thumbs... tethered–cord syndrome, spina bifida, neurogenic bladder and bowel, and a dislocated left hip with no L 5–S1 nerve. Because of this, we had to amputate his left foot so he could remain weight bearing with a prosthesis. Noah only has one kidney and is classified profoundly deaf. Noah has had over 30 major surgeries. Now he is 17 years old. Noah's dream for as long as I can remember is to meet Dan Marino...

Do you know how many wishes he has granted?

Do you have any idea how many lives Dan Marino has touched, how much joy he has brought, how much magic he has made when he wasn't on a field?

How do you quantify 17 years of this kind of giving or, more appropriately, 17 years of giving this kind?

How do you put a number on philanthropy this profound?

Do you count the millions Marino has raised for various childrens' charities?

Or the millions he has given out of his own pocket?

Do you start closer to home, with the hospital he helped build minutes from where he lives in Weston?

Or do you start in his home, with the little girl he adopted from China?

Or is the best way to appreciate the bigger picture to start by staring at something small?

"I don't need to see any Man of the Year trophies," Cindy Jarvis says. "I've seen his heart for myself."

Cindy had a surprise for her sick boy. They were going to the Dec. 19 game between the Dolphins and Chargers last season, and Noah was plenty happy with simply that. He didn't really expect to meet Marino, but he made an oil painting for him anyway, as a Christmas present. He figured he'd holler loud and long, and maybe somehow get Marino's attention as he jogged off the field afterward.

What the heck?

Noah had beaten bigger odds before, right?

So now there are five minutes left in the game, and a man in a suit walks up to Noah and tells him he needs to be somewhere else – over by the locker room, where Marino will soon meet him. Merry Christmas, Cindy tells her son, eyes watering.

"You have to understand," Cindy says now. "Noah is my miracle. I was told he would never live, never walk, never talk. But he dances, he paints..."

Cindy's voice gives up here.

"Dan Marino gave my boy the best moment of his life," she says, choking on the words. "Noah's whole face lit up meeting him. I've never seen that kind of joy on his face. He had gone to heaven. It was his dream. Dan talked to him for a really long time, and I just lost it right there. I was crying the whole time."

Marino laughed with Noah, took pictures, answered all his questions. He signed Noah's prosthesis, which Noah

With a young fan at an autograph session.

Marino hands out supplies to needy victims of Hurricane Andrew.

Photo by BILL FRAKES

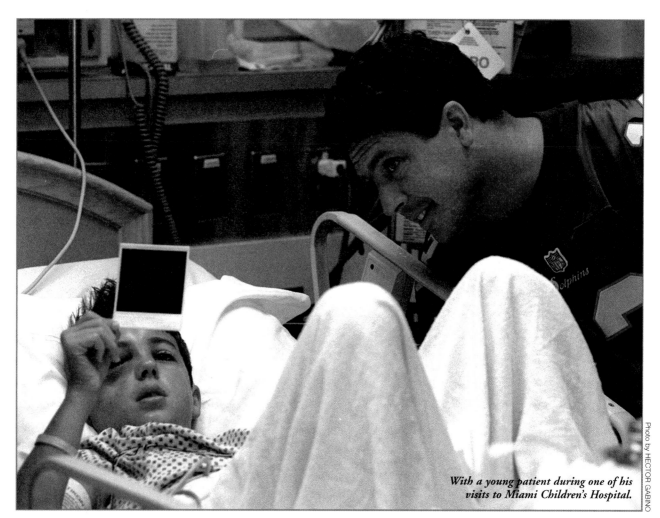

With a young patient during one of his visits to Miami Children's Hospital.

would later show off to his friends at the hospital. Today, Noah has Dolphins stuff on his bedroom curtains, on his bedspread, on his wallpaper, on his school folders. He even added Dolphins logos to the braces that help him walk. And just the other day, out of the blue, even though Marino was struggling with being rejected by a Dolphins team that no longer wanted him, Noah got something to add to his collection.

"Thank you for the beautiful oil painting," the hand–written note read. "I have a house on the water. I have the perfect wall for the painting to hang on."

Cindy Jarvis cries while reading Marino's letter.

"What a wonderful man," she says.

Dear Kathie Lee Gifford:

I need help from you and Frank. I know you help children and hope you can help here. Our friend and neighbor, Erin McCollum, *who is only 13 years old, has a rare form of brain cancer. This year, they found two tumors on her spine. Her dream and wish is to meet Dan Marino...*

Marino cries.

For 17 years, he has met dying children after games, and he has laughed with them and he has hugged them and sometimes he has cried with them, too. Marino has always been completely overwhelmed at the thought that a dying child's final wish is to meet him, of all people, which is why he pours himself into the experience so completely – never looking at his watch, never wanting to seem burdened, always answering questions until the children run out of them and then asking, "Is there anything else I can do for you?"

If you study the hundreds of photographs he has taken with sick children over his 17 years as a Dolphin, you

Photo by DAVID BERGMAN

A birthday wish from an enthusiastic fan at Pro-Player stadium.

will see a radiant Marino smiling a natural, relaxed smile that very few in South Florida have ever seen – a smile that is usually larger than even the child's. Marino smiles this way because he knows that snapshot – to be framed and frozen in forever – will probably be the way sick kids all over America will remember him for whatever remains of their lives.

All of this drains him, though, drains him like no football game he has ever played, because some of the kids are yellowed or coughing or twitching, some are missing hair or covered in sores or tumor–ridden, and Marino inevitably gets attached.

One time, for example, after a Saturday practice, Marino spent some time with a dying 17–year–old boy who, at meeting's end, gave him a golden guardian angel as a gift. To guard over you when I'm gone, the boy explained. Not wanting to cry right in front of the boy, Marino quickly took off his sweat shirt, told the boy to please wear it to the game the next day and bolted for the locker room, where he wept alone. Marino wore the angel pin on his baseball cap the rest of the season.

Erin McCollum stayed with Marino in a different way, after Kathie Lee Gifford reached Marino on behalf of the little girl's neighbor. Marino flew to Ohio to meet her one night, spending an evening with her at an Italian restaurant.

"He certainly brought a lot of happiness to that little girl, and we'll always be grateful to him for that," the girl's father, Robert, is saying now. "He was very attentive to her the whole time. She was walking on clouds for a long time after that."

Marino later sent Erin Dolphins caps for her and her classmates. He made a plan to see her again, at a Dolphins game, but after 10 hours of surgery and eight months of chemotherapy, she was too sick to make the trip. Marino, told she wasn't coming, called her unsolicited.

"Erin, it's for you," her father shouted across the house, holding up the phone. "It's Dan Marino."

"Yeah, right," her friends said.

Marino began asking Erin about her health, but she interrupted him.

Erin would pass away a few months later, but at that point she wanted to know how Marino's ankle was.

Astounded that she was worried about his health, Marino was struck silent for a moment. He composed himself enough to answer all her questions. Then, tears in his eyes, he called his wife and kids to tell them how much he loved them.

Dear Alladin:

My name is Tim Wall I have a rare bone disease kniest syndrome I live with my mom and sister. I am 12 years old. I were 2 hearing aids and a back brace to help my back straight. I get around OK but I need some help. I do have one wish and my wish is to go to Miami, Florida to see a Miami Dolphins game and meet Dan Marino. He is my favorite player, so if you could grant me one wish that would be it...

"They can do anything in the world before they die, and they choose to meet him," says Fudge Brown, the team's director of community relations. "Danny recognizes the gravity of that. It's an enormous responsibility, and it takes a kind, caring person to deal with it. The beauty of Danny has always been that he doesn't do it for anyone but the kid. Not because the TV lights are there, not because he wants to polish his image for the advertisers, not because people might be watching. It's always about sharing something with the kids."

Brown, sitting behind her desk at the team's headquarters in Davie, is asked how many such requests she receives for Marino's time.

She laughs.

She is surrounded by dozens upon dozens of files dedicated to such requests.

She pulls out just one.

Marino's Foundation gets a whole other flood of requests (an average of 25,000 a year, according to director Ralph Stringer, who isn't even counting the occasional letter from poor people asking Marino for things like $100,000), but this file in Brown's office is a good example of pleas made through the team. It is thick with hand–written notes from kids and typed letters from adults, some of them asking for help, some of them expressing gratitude for help that has already come.

One letter reads, "Today I am writing on behalf of Kerry Nielsen, a 30–year–old father of three who is nearing the end of his battle with cancer. Kerry is a huge fan of the Miami Dolphins and especially Dan Marino. Kerry and his family have never had the opportunity to attend a Dolphins game, and Kerry has asked us to grant him this last dying wish. This dream means the world to Kerry because he knows that he will not be alive for next year's season."

Another: "Awesome" is how Joel described his meeting

Photo by BILL FRAKES

The Family Man: Marino plays with son Danny in the family's backyard pool in Weston.

with Dan. He said that Saturday had been the best day of his life. Little did he know Sunday would be even better.

Another: "You made Steven feel so special by playing catch, answering all his questions, signing so many souvenirs and giving him your hat and sweatbands. As a parent, it was wonderful to watch Steven be a kid and experience such joy after all that he's been through over the past two years."

There are four requests from dying children, from a 15–year–old in Sioux City and a 6–year–old from Los Angeles who have leukemia, from an 11–year–old in Philadelphia who has muscular dystrophy and a 17–year–old from Pittsburgh who has Friedreich's ataxia – four requests from dying children in a single, one–page letter.

Fudge Brown flips through dozens of these, flips through this one file among hundreds, and says, "About 99.9 percent of our requests are for Dan. My toughest job is educating people that we have 50 other players who do this kind of work."

Only Michael Jordan, according to Brown, is requested more than Marino by the Make–A–Wish Foundation.

"Look at this picture," Brown says, thumbing through the file.

The photo is of a boy in a hospital. He is tilted back in a wheelchair, a Dolphins blanket on his lap, hands gnarled on his chest. The boy developed brain damage after spitting a ball up in the air and getting it caught in his throat. The picture shows Marino gently leaning in to touch the boy. The awed boy is staring at Marino wide–eyed, much to his nearby mother's surprise.

"I don't want to get too miraculous on you, but look at the boy's eyes," Brown says. "Would you believe this boy was completely comatose before Dan touched him? That he was completely nonresponsive to anybody until Dan touched him?"

Dear Dolphins:

Ten–year–old Ashley's special wish is to meet Dan Marino and attend the Dolphins–Patriots game Nov. 21. This youngster will be traveling from New Jersey. Her diagnosis is cerebral palsy with complications...

The Fegos are lifelong Jets fans. Gary Fego is particularly rabid, having followed the team ever since getting Joe Namath's autograph as a child. So, naturally, Ashley, their little niece with cerebral palsy, became a Dolphins fan just to annoy them. She fell in love with Miami's quarterback, who she thought was cute.

"So we figure that maybe we can get tickets to one of Dan's game's from the team, but Dan says, no, he wants to meet her personally," Judy Fego is saying now. "We couldn't believe the way he treated her, the impression that he made. He treated her like a queen. They talked about their dogs. They talked about how Ace Ventura was their favorite movie. He put his cap on her head. He waved to her after the game. He told her how beautiful she was. And he gave her hugs. Lots of hugs..."

Judy Fego pauses here, voice cracking.

"What he did for her, I can't even explain it. He gave her the thrill of her life. If you look at the video now, all me and my husband did was cry. Ashley has had 12 surgeries – on her eyes, her legs, her heart. She can't walk or see that well. And he made her feel like the most beautiful person in the world. Do you speak to him at all? Will you tell him that she still cries whenever she watches the video?"

Ashley has three copies of the video, at her house and her grandmother's and at the Fego's, so she can watch it wherever she is. Her room is aqua and white, with a Dolphins bed set and Marino posters on the wall. As for her aunt and uncle, the lifelong Jets fans, well...

"If the Dolphins and Jets are playing for the right to go to the Super Bowl," Judy Fego says, "you can bet this whole family will be rooting for Dan Marino and the Dolphins." ■

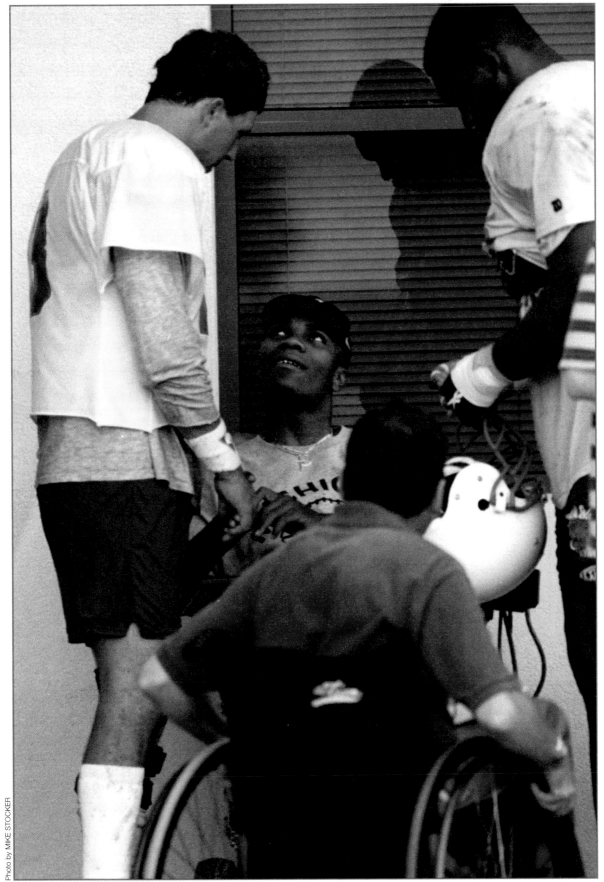

Photo by MIKE STOCKER

Kendrick English, a high school player who suffered a paralyzing injury during a game, listens to Marino's encouraging words after a Dolphins practice.

119

A Singular Focus

By Edwin Poope

Dan Marino has never been about talking. Only passing. At risk of coming off as melodramatic, I always thought the reason God put him down here specifically was to throw a football.

Of course he was also sent to be an intensely involved family man and a benevolent charitable force in the community.

Everything else about Marino, though, goes back to passing, not palaver. He walked the walk without talking the talk. Except for his family, just about everything

except passing was entirely incidental in Marino's life.

Precisely that is what Marino is all about. Precisely that is what made Marino so special as to be unique in all the history of America's most popular game.

You couldn't pry a true nugget of a quote about football out of him. Except maybe twice. And he apologized for the second.

The first surprise arrived back in the mid–1990s. For the first time, he said he was considering the awful possibility that he might complete his Hall of Fame–bound career without winning a Super Bowl.

"It's not going to keep me awake every night," he told me one spring day in the locker room.

It had to be spring because the only thing he ever talked about during season was the last game or the next one.

"Sure I'd be disappointed if that happened. That's the whole idea, to win the biggest thing there is. But," and his voice trailed away, "it could happen . . ."

The second came when he blew his top at a WSVN–TV sports announcer after the Dolphins lost to the Colts 37–34 last season.

Ducis Rodgers asked Marino "how tough" that felt. It was a fair question. It was fair because Marino had thrown three touchdown passes, and even Colts prodigy Peyton Manning had said, "It got to the point where I couldn't look on third down because Dan was putting the ball 15 yards on a rope."

Marino called the question "ridiculous." Then he really went off.

"I'll tell you how tough it is," he said, in a voice uncommonly loud for him in any postgame interview. "You work your butt off

With tears in his eyes, Marino announces his retirement after 17 seasons with the Miami Dolphins.

Photo by AL DIAZ

The unshakeable Dan Marino.

Under pressure, Marino gets a pass off against Carolina.

Photo by DAVID BERGMAN

all week and then you lose a game like that by three points with two seconds left. That's how tough it is, but you wouldn't know, would you?"

Marino later dispatched an apology to Rodgers. But he had given us a rare public glimpse of what went on inside that famous, handsome man.

I spent hundreds of hours waiting for Marino to return to his locker after games. He wouldn't talk until he had showered and at least half-dressed. By then the crowd of reporters and cameramen around his tiny space would have swelled to dozens. He talked in the softest of voices, altogether unlike the one he used to bark signals. So you were sunk unless you got there early enough to be in the first couple of rows around him. And if you did that, it meant giving up all the other player interviews.

I finally found a way to hear him one evening when I wound up four or five rows back. WTVJ-TV's Ross

Noble instructed me to plug my radio earphones into his camera.

Instant audio!

Except Marino never said anything. He tried. He just didn't internalize. He was a football creature, not a commentator, even when the subject was himself.

So others had to do it.

The best description of Marino came from Mark Clayton, who took part in a bunch of the record-breaking.

"Seems like Dan's not from here," was Clayton's line.

By "here," Clayton meant Earth, which Marino for so long seemed to fly above.

For his part, Marino would sum up performances with, "Yeah, I felt pretty good," or, conversely, "I made some bad decisions."

Yet, often, by not speaking more elaborately, Marino was doing something you could honestly call noble.

Photo by JOE RIMKUS JR

Smiling during a practice session.

Photo by AL DIAZ

Fans say farewell… and thanks.

He never slimed his defense. He had a million chances, but he never did.

Not that those defenses forced Marino's obsession with keeping the ball in the air. He would have done it no matter what. But those defenses helped keep him out of all but one Super Bowl.

Paul "Dr. Z" Zimmerman of Sports Illustrated pointed to Marino's sad part in the Dolphins' 38–16 loss to the 49ers in the 19th Super Bowl.

Zimmerman said too many of Marino's 318 yards passing came "in a flurry of gimme completions" at the end. He said two of Marino's passes to an open Nat Moore "nose–dived" and one of those hit Moore in the foot.

"Maybe... a story will come out... that Marino wasn't right..." Zimmerman went on. "That he was packing too much weight or he had arm trouble or he was still suffering the effects of a dizzy spell he'd had in Thursday's practice."

Another "or maybe" got to the heart of that hellish afternoon.

"Or maybe it was just that he didn't have the luxury of working against a Dolphin defense, as Montana did," Zimmerman wrote. "What he faced was a 49er defense that was the toughest in the NFL and that allowed only one touchdown in the playoffs – by the Dolphins."

Marino never mentioned that.

He didn't mention, either, that the Dolphins didn't have any runners remotely comparable to the 49ers' Roger Craig. He refused to knock his runners and especially the offensive line.

Can you remember Marino uttering one critical word toward his line in all those 17 years? He appreciated the pass–blocking all the time it worked, which was a pretty good while. Therefore he wouldn't fault the run–blocking.

Once, when the ground non–attack had been particularly gruesome, I mentioned it to Marino.

He looked quizzically at me, as though he had never thought of the running game as having anything to do with anything.

"Oh yeah," he finally muttered. "Maybe so. But don't blame it on them."

He wouldn't blame anything on anyone else because he always felt he could win the games himself. Oh sure, he knew he had to have the blocking and the catchers, but he never doubted for one second that he would be the one launching the game–winners. No one knew better than Marino that he was born to throw.

Someone out in Denver some time ago asked John Elway, "Who do you call the greatest?"

Elway replied, "I've always enjoyed watching Marino. By the criteria I use to judge QBs, the best would probably be Joe Montana. But I could watch Dan throw for hours."

Marino couldn't or wouldn't describe his own talents partly because he didn't trust anyone to know what he was talking about when he got into the intricacies of passing.

But the biggest reason was, passing came as naturally as breathing to him, and how do you get specific about how breathing feels?

"Throwing the ball has always been everything to Dan," Phil Simms said on a Buffalo afternoon last fall. The old Giants quarterback's son Chris, a pure freshman QB, was seeing considerable action at Texas, and I asked, "How come your boy is playing so much if he's a true freshman?"

"Because he can throw that son of a gun," Simms said, except he didn't actually say "son of a gun."

Simms laughed then. "Every time I would see Dan Marino back when my kid was coming up in high school, I would say something about Chris. And Dan would say one thing, 'Just tell me one thing – can he throw? Can he throw the ball?' That's all Dan ever wanted to know."

All he ever wanted to know, or do. ■

Photo by AL DIAZ

Looking back on a proud career, Marino manages a smile during is retirement announcement

Thousands of passes and thousands of memories like this TD pass to Tony Martin. No quarterback ever did it better.

Marino waves to an emotional crowd after his last home game as a Miami Dolphin.